The Real Philadelphia Book

JAZZ BRIDGE
THE REAL BOOK
PHILADELPHIA
2nd Edition

Temple University Press
Philadelphia • Rome • Tokyo

TEMPLE UNIVERSITY PRESS
Philadelphia, Pennsylvania 19122
tupress.temple.edu

Published 2022

∞ The paper used in this publication meets the requirements of the American National Standard for Information Sciences—Permanence of Paper for Printed Library Materials, ANSI Z39.48–1992

Printed in the United States of America

9 8 7 6 5 4 3 2 1

About ***The Real Philadelphia Book*, 2nd Edition**

A note from David Dzubinski, *concept originator and editor*

It was in 2010 that the idea for ***The Real Philadelphia Book*** flashed before me. I was organizing some of my own music for publication when I got to thinking about all the original music that must be out there by the Philadelphia jazz and blues community—all the compositions I had never heard or even seen. So much creative, innovative and historic music continually comes out of this region. How exciting would it be if there was a book or database specifically dedicated to our composers and lyricists? I decided to pursue it and took the idea to Jazz Bridge.

The aim of this book is to help the community grow deeper, stronger connections, while also serving to formally document much of the important music being created in the Philadelphia metro area by both well-known and lesser-known musicians. It is my intent to have this be a continuing entity that will be handed down to subsequent generations of our local musicians and to the world.

***The Real Philadelphia Book*, 2nd Edition,** is a small sampling from the wealth of original compositions by Philadelphia's vast music community and, as such, is also offered as an open invitation for more area composers and lyricists to contribute their work for future publication and to build the database. This book also serves as a vehicle for personal expression and collaboration; as a tool for the distribution of our artists' work for performance, recordings and licensing information; and to help maintain the great ongoing legacy of Philadelphia regional jazz and blues talent.

A note from Suzanne Cloud, *Co-founder and former Executive Director (retired) of the Jazz Bridge Project, and editor*

Jazz Bridge is very happy and honored to be included in this project. The organization has always felt that the best ideas come from the ground up, and David Dzubinski's aspiration was truly a dream that needed fulfillment. ***The Real Philadelphia Book*** enhances and adds to the rich Philadelphia jazz and blues tradition, and everyone affiliated with Jazz Bridge, including its Board of Directors, staff, volunteers, co-founders and fans, salutes the hard work done by so many to accomplish this goal. We predict the applause from the bandstand will extend well into the future!

The organization's thanks also go out to the Pew Center for Arts & Heritage; the Samuel S. Fels Fund; Temple University Press; Dr. Diane Turner, curator of the Charles L. Blockson Afro-American Collection at Temple University; Board Member Alan Lewine for his hard work on licensing issues and the final stages of project management; Kathy Ridl, graphic artist to all things jazz; and all the musicians who worked on this book and whose support and help with outreach was crucial for this project to be realized.

Jazz Bridge also acknowledges its former Executive Director Jeff Duperon and former Treasurer and Administrative Assistant Jim Miller (a great jazz drummer with a keen editorial eye) for their extensive efforts on this project. Jazz Bridge dedicates this edition of ***The Real Philadelphia Book*** to their memories.

Acknowledgments

This expanded second edition of ***The Real Philadelphia Book*** is the culmination of more than a decade's work in assembling, cataloging, transcribing, engraving and licensing the hundreds of compositions it contains. Over several years, many people worked on the original first edition of ***The Real Philadelphia Book***, none harder than editor *David Dzubinski*, who was the originator of the idea and spent many anxious days and sleepless nights cataloging the many submissions, developing a rubric for the evaluation panel to apply to the music, and then coordinating the formatting of the final choices with a group of musicians who volunteered to see the project through in various roles: *Don Glanden*, *Jason Fifield*, *Kaylé Brecher*, *Jeff Baumeister* and *Suzanne Cloud*. Other musicians who prepared the lead sheets from handwritten charts or directly from audio versions include *Jason Long*, *Jay Fluellen*, *Dimitri Angelakis*, *Greg Toro*, *Tom Glenn* and *David Middleton*. Many thanks to the composers on the evaluation panel—*Aaron Graves*, *Monnette Sudler*, *Bill Jolly*, *Tom Lawton* and *Don Glanden*—who lent their ears to the overwhelming number of submissions, and to the late drummer *Jim Miller* for his expert research and copyediting skills. Many thanks to graphic artist and musician *Kathy Ridl* for her loving work gathering the project together for printing and to *Don Sickler* at *Second Floor Music* for his assistance with licensing clearances. Lastly, to all the contributing composers for recognizing the inherent potential of *David Dzubinski*'s visionary concept: Thanks for wanting to be a part of ***The Real Philadelphia Book*, 2nd Edition.**

Jazz Bridge is indebted to the following funders who helped get this project off the ground: the *Pew Center for Arts & Heritage*; the *Samuel S. Fels Fund*; *Homer Jackson* and the *Philadelphia Jazz Project*; *Owlsong Productions*; and especially *Temple University Press*.

For more information on ***The Real Philadelphia Book*, 2nd Edition,** visit www.jazzbridge.org.

Contents

Composer Index

Cloud, Suzanne	Collagen Lips
	Juste un Peu de Chance
	A Lullaby, Dear Monk
Colligan, Robert	Sam Meets James
Colombo, Paul	Rio Crystal
D'Amico, Emile	Matt's Blues
D'Amico, "Father" John	3-D Blues
	Josephine
David, Norman	Give Me the Ball
	It's Always There
Davis, Matt	In Waves
	Transcendence
Davis, William R., Jr.	Solomon's Serenade
DeFrancesco, Joey	Peace Bridge
	Project Freedom
	The Unifier
Dragoni, Jim	The Wicked Prosper
Drewes, Doug	Green
Dzubinski, David	Inspired by Highest Reason
	Wonders Unfold
Eldred, Sandy	Just Remembered
Eubanks, Duane	Beer and Water
	Dance with Aleta
Eubanks, Robin	Victory
Fambrough, Charles	Little Man
Fanelli, Bob	Frank
Faulk, Adam	Sunday Blues
Fearrington, Rhenda	This Moment's Sweetness
Fifield, Jason	S'Life
Fluellen, Jay	Blueprint the Sky
	He Walks among Us
	The One Who Heals
Fraticelli, Jason	These Are the Good Ol' Days
Gahnt, Ella	Let It Be Yesterday
Gairo, Tony	Elusivity
Galante, Gloria	Bellissima
Gehman, Paul	Quid Pro Quo
Gibbs, Doc	Baila Pammi
	Hilda's Lullaby
Giess, Paul	Prayer for Mimi

Kobie, Jawanza	After the Show
Kramer, Mark	Sunday Afternoon
	Troubled Times
Krolak, Nicholas	All That Is Before You
Lalasis, Andy	Ballet
	The Opener
Lancaster, Byard	Keno
	Mr. AA
Lanza, Lou	Nightingale
Larsson, Monika	Teardrops for Jimmy
Lawton, Fran	The Ruling Passion
	The Self I Used to Be, but Never Knew I Was, and Now I Am Again
Lawton, Tom	Bechet-like
	Darwinian Swirl
	Dig the Chartreuse
Levin, Elliott	Jazz-o-etry to Complete Communion
	Soul-Etude
Lewine, Alan	Miles Away
Long, Jason	Departing Westbound
	Tap Shoe Blues
Lordi, Michelle	Scare the Ghost
Lowry, Zoe	Obsessive
Luca, AJ	Seek First
Mallon, Vincent	Code Blue
Marsceill, Christopher	Isla's Waltz
Martino, Pat	Inside Out
	Lean Years
	On the Midnight Special
Masri, Julius	Tactical Strategies no. 1
McBride, Christian	Brother Mister
	The Shade of the Cedar Tree
	The Wizard of Montara
McKenna, Larry	Is It Over My Head?
	One Falling Tree
	Perhaps This Wintertime
Meashey, Kelly	Mother Tree
Meek, William	Ballad 1
	Dusk
Merritt, Jymie	Nommo
Mesterhazy, George	My Love
Miceli, Tony	Vince Guaraldi
	What's That?
Miller, Jim	Serendib Lasio
	Suzy's Upright

Salemyr, Per	Saying Goodbye
Santos, Raimundo	So Smile
	To Be
Sarles, Randy	Mother Tree
Scott, Shirley	Oasis
Shuster, Bob	First Dance
Siet, J.	Warm Embraces
Simmons, James "Sid"	Keep the Faith
Simon, John David	Inwood
	Saying Goodbye
Simon, Wendy	Loony Blues
	My Kind of Blues
Smith, Lee	My Kind of Blues
	The Promise
Snyder, Greg	Rapids
Souponetsky, Kat	Sasha's Song
Speller, Keno	Mr. AA
Straczynski, Joe	Lovelife
Strawitz, Steve	Pack 'n Roll
Sudler, Monnette	Come to Me
	Lemar Shongo
	Other Side of the Gemini
Sutin, Benjamin	Tangibility
Swana, John	Loony Blues
	Ortlieb's
Swanson, Rob	Aria's Late Night Session
Tampio, Vince	Slimery
Taylor, Dylan	Art, the Messenger
Timmons, Bobby	So Tired
Tonooka, Sumi	Mingus Mood
Vale, Keli	Love Is to Blame
Valentino, Johnnie	This Way Out
Vanore, John	Bunk
Walker, Johnny	Advent
Washington, Grover, Jr.	East River Drive
	Let It Flow
Wilson, Dave	Smooth Sailing
	Spiral
Wolters, Arlyn	I Call It Love
Yaple, Matt	Evening Song
Yellen, E. J.	Katy's Song
Zankel, Bobby	The Next Time I See You
	We Miss You Sadly

3-D Blues

"Father" John D'Amico

Recorded on : ""Father" John D'Amico Trio Live at the Painted Bride"/Encounter Audiophile Records Services, Inc., (EARS-1006)
Remastered 1999, Dreambox Media

Advent

Recorded on: Johnny Walker "Advent"/Walk-On Records, 1982

After the Show
Medium Up Tempo
♩ = 146
Jawanza Kobie
A
Ami7(9) Gmi7 Dmi7
Ebmi7 Em7 Fm7(b5) Gbmi7 Gmi7(add11) Abmi7
1.
2.
Abmi7 Ami7
Solo - [pno- swing]
B
Ami7 Gmi7 Ami7
Ami7 Gmi7 Ami7
Dmi7 Ebmi7 Dmi7 Ami7 Dmi7 Ebmi7 Dmi7 Ami7
Emi7 Ebmi7 Dmi7 Ebmi7 Emi7 Ebmi7 Emi7 Ebmi7 Dmi7 Ebmi7 Emi7 Ebmi7
Emi7 Ebmi7 Dmi7 Ebmi7 Emi7 Ebmi7 Dbma7
Solos
Emi7 Dmi7 Dmi7 G7 G7 Cmi7

53 A♭ma7 Ami7(♭5) D7 G7 A♭7 G7
61 Emi7 Dmi7 A♭ma7 D♭ma7
69 G♭ma7 B(sus4) Emi7 Dmi7 Emi7
77 Emi7 E♭mi7 Dmi7 E♭mi7 Emi7 E♭mi7 Emi7 E♭mi7 Dmi7
80 E♭mi7 Emi7 E♭mi7 Emi7 E♭mi7 Dmi7 E♭mi7 Emi7 E♭mi7
83 D♭ma7 D♭ma7 Ami7(add9)
87 Gmi7 Dmi7
90 E♭mi7 Em7 Fm7(♭5) G♭mi7 Gmi7(add11) A♭mi7
93 Ami7(add9) Gmi7
96 Dmi7 E♭mi7 Emi7 Fmi7(♭5) G♭mi7 A♭mi7 Ami7

All That Is Before You

Nicholas Krolak

Anysha

Trudy Pitts

Recorded on: Trudy Pitts "These Blues of Mine"/Prestige, 1967
http://musicians.allaboutjazz.com/trudypitts

April Fooling

Aria's Late Night Session

Recorded on: Rob Swanson "My Bassic Hats"
www.robswansonmusic.com

Art, the Messenger

Dylan Taylor

Recorded on: Dylan Taylor "Sweeter for the Struggle"/Miles Records, 2013/Fortunebaby Music BMI
www.dylantaylor.com

Ash Wednesday March

Form: Intro- rhythm section
Head and Solos- AABB
Cadenza- rhythm section improvises
All play last chord

Recorded on: Minas "In Rio"/2006
www.minasmusic.com

Ashley and Juliet

Sean J. Kennedy

Easy Jazz Waltz- Lullaby

Recorded on: The Sean J. Kennedy Quartet "Road to Wailea (Deluxe Edition)"
www.seanjkennedy.com

Baila Pammi

© Leonard "Doc" Gibbs/Cliff Starkey
Recorded on: Doc Gibbs & Picante "Servin' It Up Hot"/Cliff Starkey Music/BMI

Ballad 1

William Meek

Ballet

Andy Lalasis & John Mulhern

Recorded on: Andy Lalasis "Fret Not"

48
E♭6/9 D♭ma13(♯11) E♭6/9 D♭ma13(♯11)
52
Cmi Cmi(ma7) Cmi7 Cmi6 A♭ma7
57
Dmi11 G7 Cmi7 F7 A♭/B♭ B♭7
62
A♭/B♭ B♭7 A/B B7 A/B
67
B7 E6/9 Dma13(♯11) E6/9 Dma13(♯11)
72
E♭6/9 D♭ma13(♯11) E♭6/9 D♭ma13(♯11) Fmi7
77
Gmi7 Ami7(♭5) Bmi7(♭5) E6/9 A♭ma(♭9)
82
E6/9 A♭ma(♭9) E6/9 A♭ma(♭9) E6/9
87
A♭ma(♭9)
[Dictated]
E♭ B A♭ E E♭ B A♭ E
E♭ma7(♯11)
fine

Bechet-like

New Orleans/Freddy Green ♩s
Tom Lawton
♩=104
Dmi6 Gmi6 Dmi6 A+7
A
Dmi6 Gmi6 Dmi/F E7 Eb7
Dmi6 C#mi7 Cmi7 F7(b9) Bbma7
E7 Eb7(b5) 1. Emi7(b5) A7(b9) 2. Emi7(b5) F#7 Bmi6 Emi6/B Bmi6
B
Fmi6 Bbmi6 Fmi6 G7 Cmi6 Do7 Cmi6/Eb D7 G+7
Abma7 Gmi7 Fmi7 Ebma7 Dbma7 Cmi7 Db7 Do7 F#/C# C#7(sus4) C#7
F#7 B/F# F# C7 F7(b9) Bmi6 C7
(Straight) Ebmi6 Bmi6 (Swing) Bb11(b9no3) Ema7(#11) A7(b9 b5)

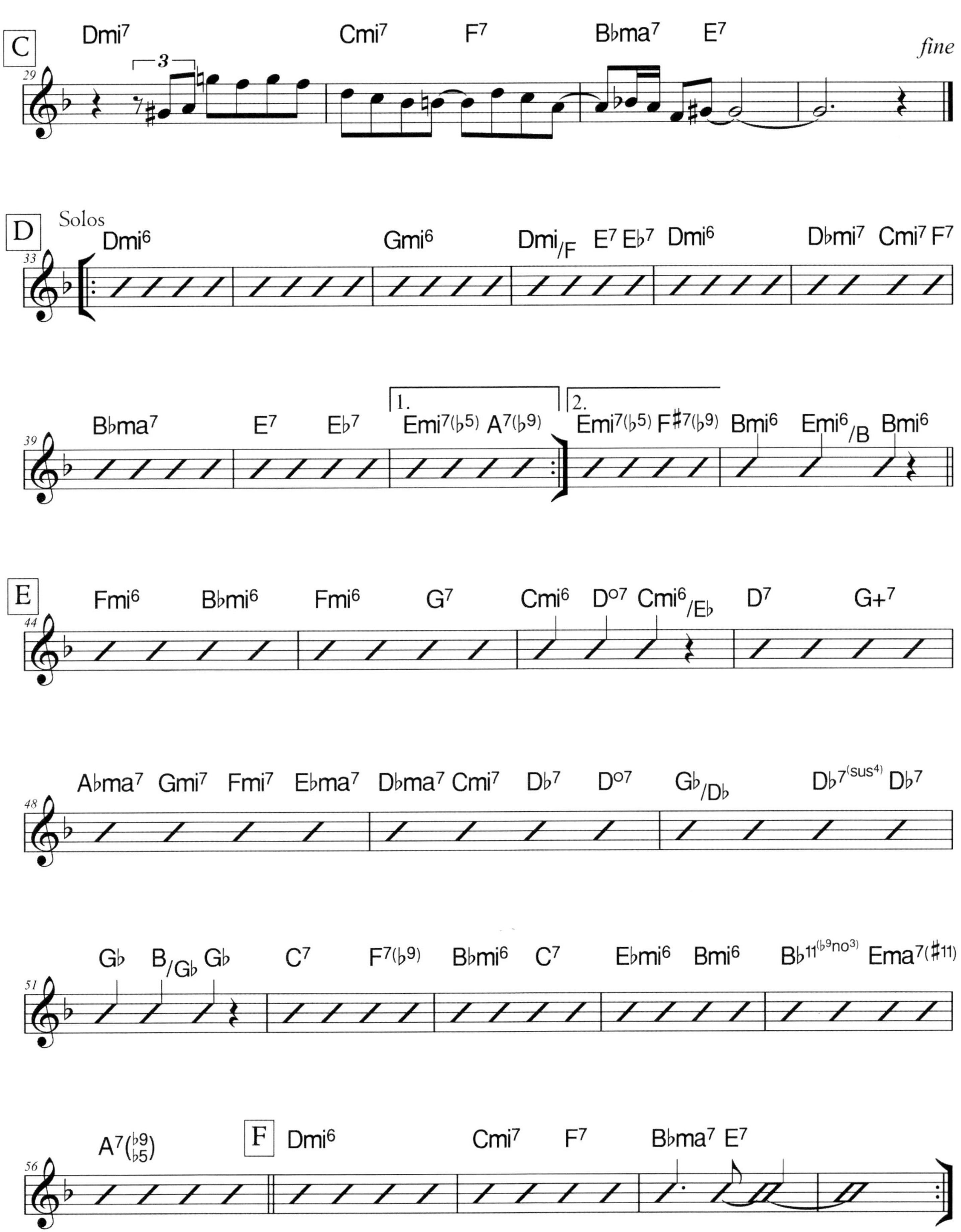
C
Dmi7 Cmi7 F7 Bbma7 E7
fine
D
Solos
Dmi6 Gmi6 Dmi/F E7 Eb7 Dmi6 Dbmi7 Cmi7 F7
Bbma7 E7 Eb7
1. Emi7(b5) A7(b9)
2. Emi7(b5) F#7(b9) Bmi6 Emi6/B Bmi6
E
Fmi6 Bbmi6 Fmi6 G7 Cmi6 Do7 Cmi6/Eb D7 G+7
Abma7 Gmi7 Fmi7 Ebma7 Dbma7 Cmi7 Db7 Do7 Gb/Db Db7(sus4) Db7
Gb B/Gb Gb C7 F7(b9) Bbmi6 C7 Ebmi6 Bmi6 Bb11(b9no3) Ema7(#11)
A7(b9 b5)
F
Dmi6 Cmi7 F7 Bbma7 E7

Beer and Water

Recorded on: Duane Eubanks "Things of That Particular Nature"/Sunnyside Records, 2015
www.duaneeubanks.com

Bell

Open Swing feel

Mike Kennedy

Recorded on: Mike Kennedy "Insulation"/Flying Feet
www.kennedymusic.com

Cma9/E Fma9 B♭ma9/A E♭/D
D♭9(♯11) B♭mi9/C B7(♭5) A♭mi9/B♭ A7(♭5)
G♭mi9/A♭ Gmi7 F(sus4)
fine
Cma9/E A♭ma13 Gmi7/D
A♭ma13 G7(sus4) Cma9/E A♭ma13
Gmi7/D A♭ma9 G7(sus4) Cma9/E B♭ma9/D A♭(add9)/C
A♭(add9)/C Gmi7 A♭ma9 F/A E♭ma7/G
F(sus4) F/A E♭ma7/G F(sus4) F/A
E♭ma7/G F(sus4) F/A E♭ma7/G F(sus4)
D.C. al fine

Bellissima

Dedicated to Danielle Galante

Gloria Galante

Recorded on: "Kusangala"/Nirvana Music/BMI
www.gloriagalante.com

Beneath the Surface

Recorded on: Mike Boone Quartet "Beneath the Surface"/Truth Revolution Records

Bless This Mouse

Recorded on: Posmontier Brothers Quintet "PBQ"/Bands Not Bombs Productions
www.daveposmontier.com

Blueprint the Sky

Jay Fluellen

♩ = ca. 160

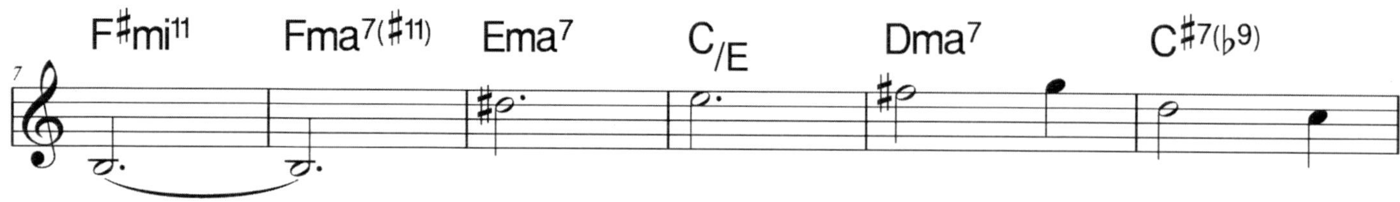

B♭6(♯11) Fma7 A-11 B-11 F♯mi7 C♯mi9
34

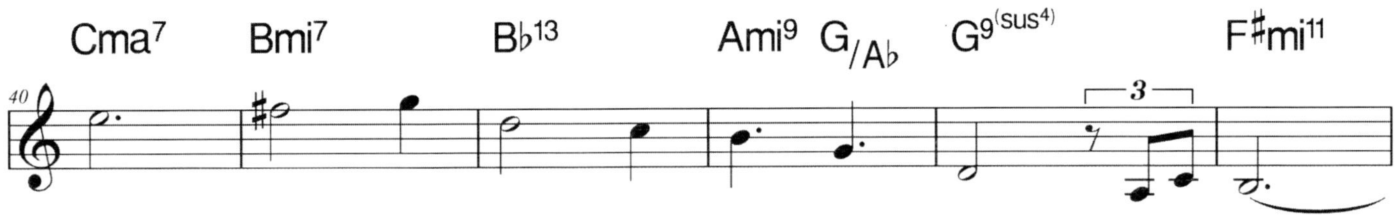
Cma7 Bmi7 B♭13 Ami9 G/A♭ G9(sus4) F♯mi11
40
3

Fma7(♯11) Ema7 C/E Dma7 C♯7(♭9) Cma7 B7(♯9)
46

Dmi9 E+7 F6 Ami11 Bmi11 F♯mi9
52

Solos over form, D.C. al Coda to End

(Last time only)
F6 Ami11 Bmi11 F♯mi7 C♯mi7
57

Ama7(♯11) Ami7(add11) Gma7/A Dmi7(♭5)/A
62

Blues for My Father

Jordan Brysk

Solos over A and B. To End play C then A and B to fine.

Recorded on: Jordan Brysk "Blues for My Father"/BMI
www.sites.google.com/site/jampaband

Blues for Trayvon

Bert Harris

www.bertbassie.com

Boogaloo Sub

Sean J. Kennedy

Medium Funky Blues

Recorded on: Sean J. Kennedy Quartet (featuring Bob Mintzer) "Road to Wailea (Deluxe Edition)" and "Queen Anne's Revenge"
www.seanjkennedy.com

Book Faded Brown

Rudimental Marching Drum

Music & Lyrics
Paul Jost

Recorded on: Paul Jost "Breaking Through"/Dot Time Records
www.pauljostmusic.com

Book Faded Brown - 2

A6/9 E(add9)/ D(add9)/F♯ E A♭+7(♭9)/E♭
By the way have I told you al-ready that his

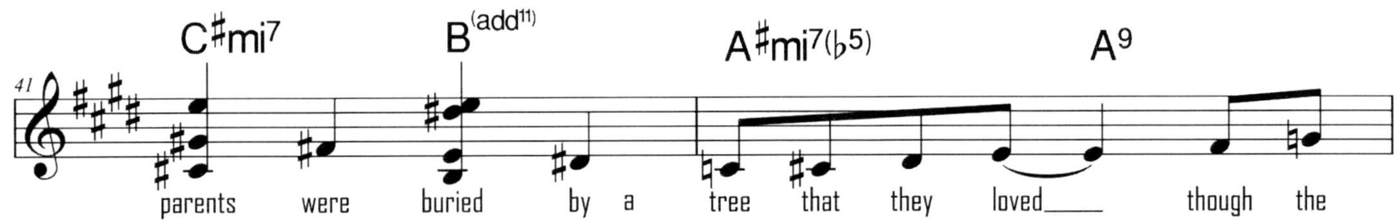
C♯mi7 B(add11) A♯mi7(♭5) A9
parents were buried by a tree that they loved___ though the

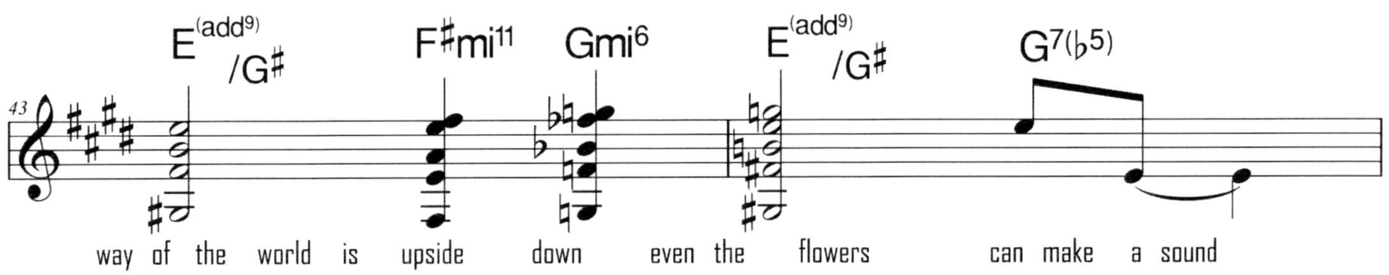
E(add9)/G♯ F♯mi11 Gmi6 E(add9)/G♯ G7(♭5)
way of the world is upside down even the flowers can make a sound

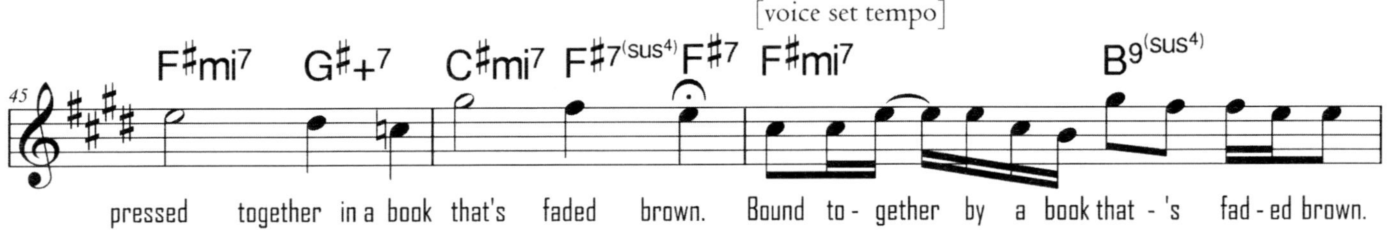
[voice set tempo]
F♯mi7 G♯+7 C♯mi7 F♯7(sus4) F♯7 F♯mi7 B9(sus4)
pressed together in a book that's faded brown. Bound to - gether by a book that - 's fad - ed brown.

E C♯mi7 Cue next E C♯mi7 E
fine
grand ritard

The Box

Recorded on: Dave Burrell and David Murray "Brother to Brother"/Gazell Records, 1993
www.daveburrell.com

BP with the GM

Music & Lyrics
Edward T. Morgan, Jr.

Recorded on: Eddie Morgan Quintet "BP with the GM"

Brother Mister

♩=132

Christian McBride

Recorded on: "Kind Of Brown"/2009
www.christianmcbride.com

Bucket Full of Soul

Recorded on: Trudy Pitts "A Bucket Full of Soul"/Prestige, 1967

Bud

Music & Lyrics
Tom Adams

D♭ma7 Fmi(♭5) B♭7(♭9)
21
cre - at - ing mel - o - dies sub - lime.
E♭9(♯11) E♭9 F13(sus4) F13
23
Mo - ving through space. Mo - ving through time.
C
B♭6/9 D♭9 G♭13 F13
25
When on the stand, the man be - hind the grand was the
Dmi7 G7(♭9) Cmi7 F13 Fmi9 E7(♯9)
27
mas- ter, of mo - dern jazz pi - a - no. A brave swing- in' heart, that
E♭6/9 D7(♯9 ♯5) C9 F13(♭9) B♭6/9
30
set him high a - part then sud - den - ly said a - dieu
Interlude (optional intro)
D
E♭mi6/9 C♭9(♯11)
33
C♭9(♯11) E♭mi6/9
35
E♭mi6/9 C♭9(♯11)
38

[*] Use quartal voicing on F chord

Recorded on: John Vanore & Abstract Truth "Blue Route"/Acoustical Concepts Records AC-15
www.johnvanore.net

BYOB

Recorded on: Chili's Choice "Prehumous"/ASCAP
www.koreyriker.com

Candlelight

Music & Lyrics
Steve Giordano

www.stevegiordanoguitar.com

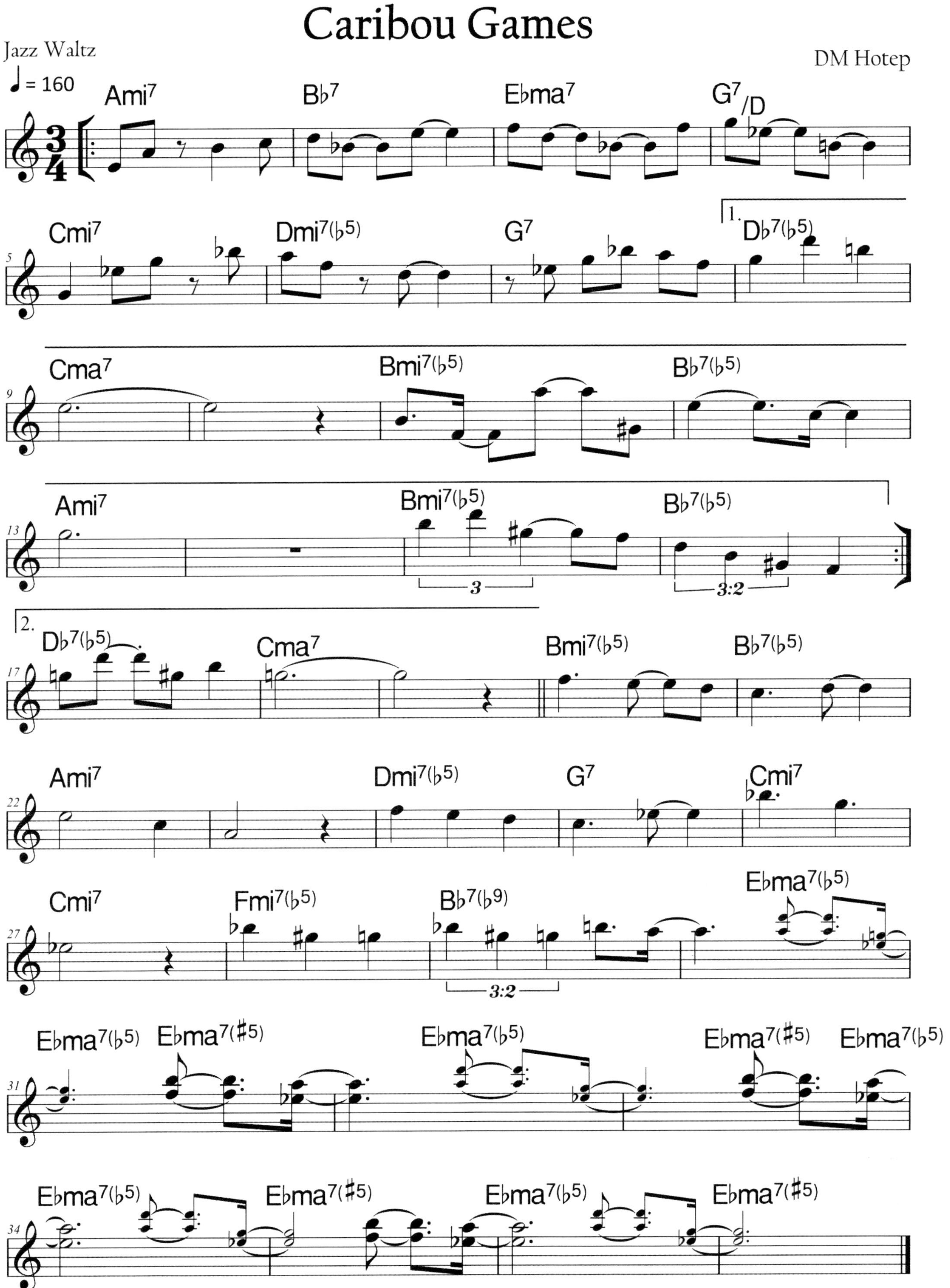

www.musicians.allaboutjazz.com/dhotep

Code Blue

Vincent Mallon

Recorded on: Vince Mallon "Vignettes"/Mallon Publishing
www.vincemallon.com

Bmi7
C♯mi7
Bmi7
C♯mi7
cof- fee__ brewed. Take one step then an-oth-er___ on the road___ to re
Bmi7
Ama7
E7(♯9)
Ama7
co-ve-ry___ from you. Code___ Blue.___
G13
Ama7
B♭13
Ama7
D9
Code___ Blue.___
Ama7
D9
Ama7
D9
Ama7
D9
C
C♯mi7
Bmi7
C♯mi7
Bmi7
Skirt too short._ I know you hate health food. Mi-nutes late,_ a blood feud-en___ sued.
C♯mi7
Bmi7
C♯mi7
Bmi7
Sleeves are long__ to hide my tat__ too.__ Sneak a smoke. It's time to say, "A___ dieu."
C♯mi7
Bmi7
C♯mi7
Bmi7
Take one step then an-oth-er___ on the road___ to re-co-ve-ry___ from
Ama7
E7(♯9)
Ama7
G13
Ama7
you. Code___ Blue.___ Code___ Blue.___
B♭13
Ama7
D9
Ama7
D9
Repeat and fade out ad lib

Code Blue - 2

Collagen Lips

Music & Lyrics
Suzanne Cloud

Medium Swing

Verse 2:

Injected fat./ Peeled my face,
Electrolisized my legs.
Lashes dyed./ My tummy's tucked.
Plastic pins hold up my butt.
A saline implant's in my chin./ You know I'm
Barbie, baby, and you're my Ken.

Verse 3:

Tattooed brows./ Crunchy hair,
Fixed all the flaws that never were there.
Permanent pink or painted toes,
Burned a mile off./ Bobbed the nose.
I'll never age. My waist won't bend, /Because I'm
Barbie, baby, and you're my Ken.

Recorded on: Suzanne Cloud "With a Little Help from My Friends"
www.dreamboxmedia.com

Come to Me

Recorded on: "Let The Rhythm Take You"/MSM-Phillyinde
www.monettesudlermusic.com

Eb(sus4) Gb/Ab Eb11 Dbma7/Bb Cmi7
21
things I feel_ in - side_ Come to me Stay_with me a - while. Come to

Dbma7/Bb Gmi7 C7(#5 b9) Dbma7 Cmi7 Bbmi7
25
me 3 I wan-na make you smile. You know I bright-en up__your day__ so why don't

Dbma7 Db/Eb Abma7 Bbmi7 Abma7 Bbmi7 Abma7 Bbmi7
28
you stay an - oth - er day

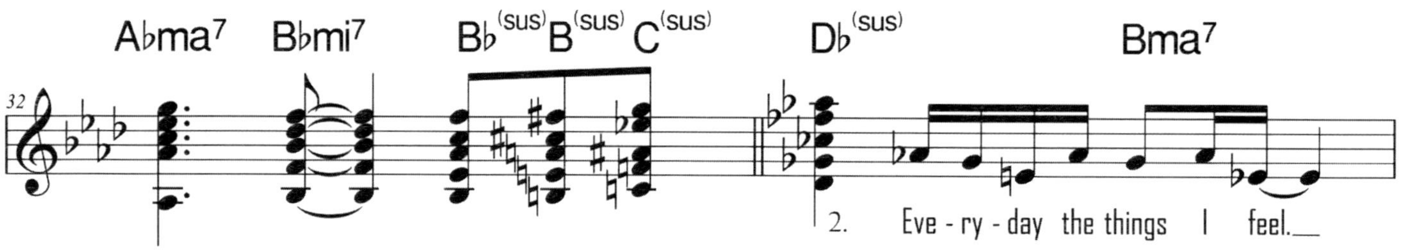
Abma7 Bbmi7 Bb(sus) B(sus) C(sus) Db(sus) Bma7
32
2. Eve - ry - day the things I feel.__

Bma7 Bb(sus) Abma7 Abmi7 Gbma7
34
3
take on a dif-fer-ent shape. one thing's cer-tain two's for sure_

Ema7 Ama7(b5) Gbma7 Bma7 Abma7
38
that I__ sure - ly__ could not__ ev - er dare es - cape.__

Db/Eb Abma7
41
Cause I have fall - en__ Fall - en so in -

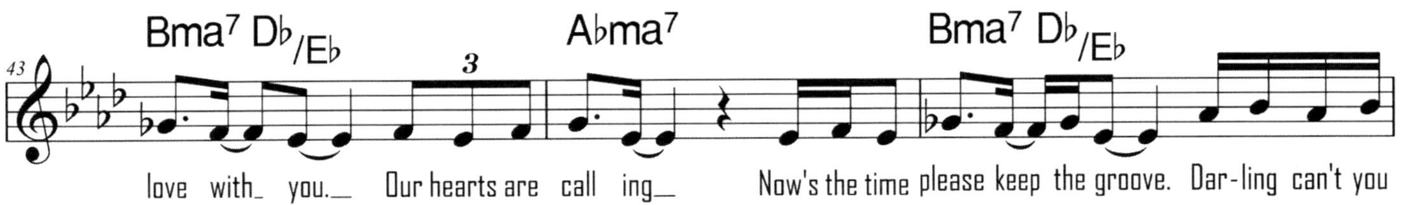
43
Bma7 Db/Eb
Abma7
Bma7 Db/Eb
3
love with_ you._ Our hearts are call ing_ Now's the time please keep the groove. Dar-ling can't you

46
Dbma7 Cmi7
Dbma7 Cmi7 Bbmi7
Eb(sus)
Gb/Ab
3
see what's in my heart___let's take the mo-ment let's_ not part_ I want you by_ my side__

49
Db/Eb
Dbma7/Bb
Cmi7
Dbma7/Bb
3
Come to me Stay_with me a - while. Come to me___ I wan-na

53
Gmi7
C7(#5 b9)
Dbma7 Cmi7
Bmi7
Dbma7 Db/Eb
make you smile. You know I bright-en up__your day__ so why don't you stay an-oth - er

56
Abma7 Bbmi7
Abma7 Bbmi7
Abma7 Bbmi7 Dbma7 Db/Eb
day.___ stay an-oth - er day.__ stay an-oth - er day.

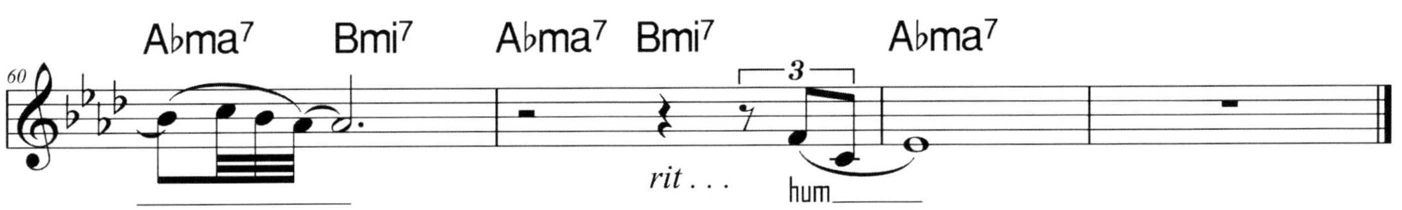
60
Abma7 Bmi7
Abma7 Bmi7
Abma7
3
rit . . .
hum___

Corojo

Dave Renz

Recorded on: The Acoustic Groove Project Album "Plugged In"
www.daverenz.com

Bbmi7
C7(b9)
Bbmi7
C7(b9)
25
Last time to coda
Fmi
Eb7
Db7(#11)
C7(b9)
Bbmi7
Ab6
Bbmi7
C7(b9)
29
Fmi7
Eb7
Db7(#11)
C7(b9)
Bbmi7
Ab7+
Fmi
33
Fmi7
Eb7
Db7(#11)
C7(b9)
Bbmi7
Ab7+
Fmi7
C7(b9)
37
Fmi7
Eb7
Db7(#11)
C7(b9)
Bbmi7
Ab7+
Fmi7
C7(b9)
41
Fmi7
Eb7
Db7(#11)
C7(b9)
Bbmi7
Ab7+
Fmi7
45

Corojo - 2

Cosby's Capers

Robert "Bootsie" Barnes

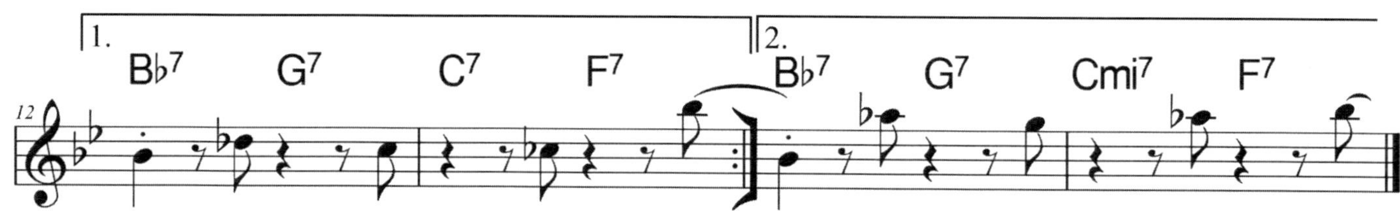

Recorded on: Bootsie Barnes "Boppin' Around the Center"/Harvest
www.bootsiebarnes.com

Dance with Aleta

Duane Eubanks

Recorded on: Duane Eubanks "Things Of That Particular Nature"/Sunnyside Records, 2015
www.duaneeubanks.com

Dance with Me

Easy Swing

Robert A. Barboni

Darwinian Swirl *

* For a more complete/specific bass part please contact the composer at: mail@dreamboxmedia.com

C♯mi/G
Fmi(ma7)
A♭mi(ma7)
Bmi(ma7)
cresc.
A/B♭
A♭/E
G/E♭
B♭
D♭ma7(♯9)
3
p
D♭ma7(♯9)
Dmi6
A♭/E
Fill (especially drums)
subito pp
Bmi(ma7)
B♭mi(ma7)
A♭/C
Fmi7
E♭7/G
A♭
E7(♯9)
[Tempo feeling of time suspended
but actually in tempo]
(except fermata)
D
[interpret]
Ami7
E♭mi7(ma7)
Gmi7
arpeggio
Gmi7
C♯mi(ma7)
Dma7(♯5)
Dma7(♯5)
Coda last time only
Dma7(♯5)
Pulsation and activity . . .
D♭7
to solos
E♭
Pedal . . . spacey in time getting softer eventually
not time to set up quiet "out" transition to end.

Departing Westbound

Up Tempo Swing

Jason Long

Recorded on: Jason Long "I Watch the Planes Go By"

Dig the Chartreuse

Recorded on: Tom Lawton "Retrospective/Debut"/Dreambox Media

C+7
C♯mi7
Bma7(♯11)
Dma7

C
Gma9
B7
D♭7(♭9)
F♯/D

Bma7/D♯
E+
B♭ma7/F♯
To Coda last time only

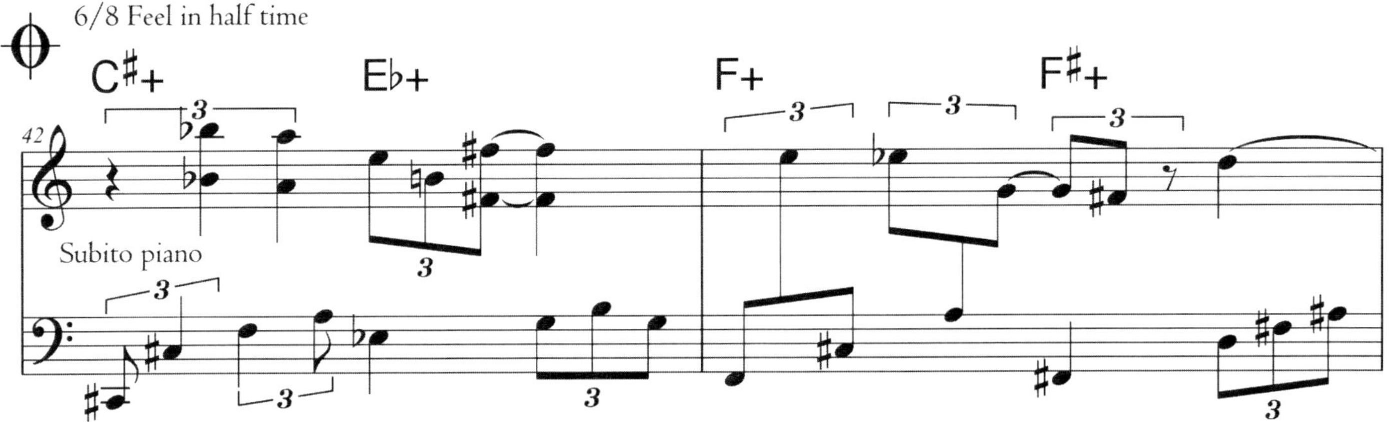
6/8 Feel in half time
C♯+
E♭+
F+
F♯+
Subito piano

Swing tempo I
[with extensions]
G/B
B♭mi7
Fmi7(ma7)
Fo7
fine

Recorded on: Dave Hartl & Gaijin "Foreign Growth"/Foaming at the Ear Music
www.davehartl.com

Solo-I
B
Ebma9
Ema7b5
Ebma9
Bma9
Cue next
C
Eb11
Db11
C11
Bb11
Fma7
Fma7
Dbma7(b5)
Fma7
Dbma7(b5)
Cma7
Fmi11
Ebma7
Ama7/C# C#mi9
Ab11
Ab7
F7(#11)
Dma7
Bbma7(b5)
Dma7
Bbma7(b5)
Solo-2
Dma9
Ebma7b5
Dma9
Cue 2nd ending
1.
Bbma9
2.
[Eb lydian]
D.S. al Coda
Dma7
Ebma7(b5)
Dma7
Bbma7
Cue next
Dma7
Ebma7(b5)
fine

Dr. D

Jim Holton

Dusk

Latin feel

William Meek

21
Fmi7 Bb7 Fmi7 D7 Dbma7 Bbmi7 Gmi7 C7+

25
Fmi7 Bb7 Db7 C7+ Fmi7 Bb7 Fmi7 Bb7

29
Ebmi7 Ab7 Dbma7 Dmi7(b5) G7 Cmi7 F7 Gmi7 G7+

33
Cmi7 G7+/B Bbmi7 Eb7 Ab6 Bb/C Fmi7 Ab7

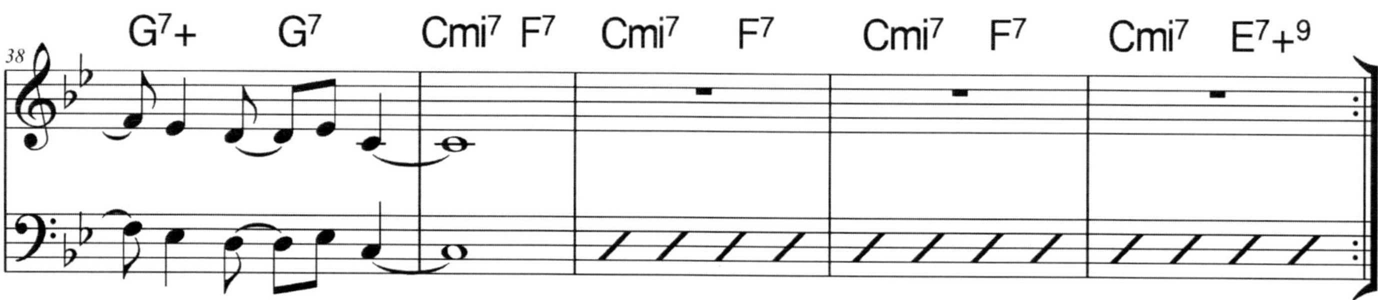
38
G7+ G7 Cmi7 F7 Cmi7 F7 Cmi7 F7 Cmi7 E7+9

East River Drive

Grover Washington, Jr.

Slow Rubato

2.
Cmi7 F Gmi6 C7 Gmi7 C7 Gmi7 C7
Solos
Gmi7 C7
16x
Fmi7 B♭7 E♭ma7 D7(♯9) G7 Cma7
Cmi7 Dmi7 E♭ma7 Dmi7 Cmi7 D7(♯9) Gmi7 C7
Gmi7 C7 Gmi7 C7 Gmi7 C7
D.S. al Coda
Cmi7 F Gmi7 C7 Gmi7 C7
Gmi7 C7 Gmi7 C7
Ad lib and fade out . . .

Elusivity

Tony Gairo

Medium Swing

Recorded on: Tony Gairo-Gary Rissmiller Jazz Orchestra "Treacherous"/Sea Breeze Records/SB-2136
www.tonygairo.com

Dmi7/E♭ Gmi7/A♭ Fma7/G E♭ma7/F Dma7/E A13(♭9)
D13(♯9) G9(♭13) Cmi9 D♭ma9
C
A♭13 Fmi7/G♭ Cmi7/F D♭/E♭ Cmi7/F Dmi/G
Solos
Cmi9 B♭9(sus4) Cmi9 B♭9(sus4)
E♭ma9 A♭ma9 Cmi9 B♭9(sus4) Ami9 D9 Gmi7 C7
Fma9 E♭7(♭9) Dm11 D♭13(♯11) G♭ma9 F9
B♭ma9 D♭7(♭9) Cmi9 B♭9(sus4)
Cmi9 B♭9(sus4) Cmi9 B♭9(sus4) G7(♭9)
after solos D.C. al Coda
Cmi11

Evening Song

Matt Yaple

"F" Street

Marc Adler

Recorded on: Marc Adler "Flute Improvisations"
www.adlerjazz.com

Falling Short... Redeemed Again

Recorded on: Kendrah E. Butler-Waters "Faith Walk"/BMI
www.kendrahbw.com

First Dance

Bob Shuster

Recorded on: Neil Wetzel "Misunderestimated"/Hot Apple Spider Productions
www.hotapplespider.com

Fleetin' Blues II

(Dubois' Ditty)

Swingin' with Attitude

Diane Monroe

Recorded on: Diane Monroe "Alone Together"
www.dianemonroemusic.com

13
G7
B♭7
16
B♭7
E♭7
18
D7
G7
21
A♭7(sus4)
C7(sus4)
A♭7(sus4)
G7(sus4)
25
A♭7(sus4)
E♭7(sus4)
D♭7(sus4)
D7

G7
B♭7
B♭7
E♭7
D7
G7
1st time, (solos) & (to head out)
Play for head out
Last time to end
G7
E♭7
D7
G7
G7
Collective Jam Out
Fade Out

Frank

Recorded on: Bob Fanelli "Heads and Tales"/Inconsensus Music
www.bobfanellimusic.com

Funkfoot

John Blake, Jr.

By John Blake

Recorded on: Kaylé Brecher "This Is Life"/Penchant Four Records
www.brecherjazz.com

Gingerbread Boy

Medium-Swing

Jimmy Heath

B♭7 B♭7(♯9)

(rhythm)

6 E♭7 E7 E♭7 B♭7(♯9)

10 B♭7 G7 C7 F7

14 B♭7(♯9)

Gingerbread Boy is a 16-bar modified blues song. Solos are over a standard 12-bar blues progression. It was originally played with a medium-swing. In bars 11 and 12, the lower octave notes are the original melody. The upper octave notes are provided in case the lower notes are below your range.

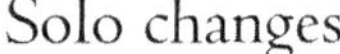

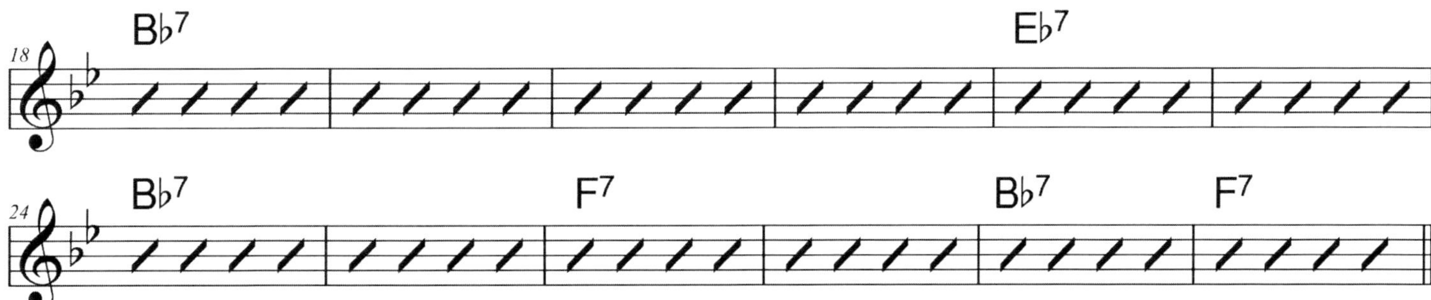

Give Me the Ball

Medium Swing

Norman David

Glad Bag

Music & Lyrics
Kaylé Brecher

Recorded on: Kaylé Brecher "Choices" (1991) and "Kayleidoscope" (2019)/Penchant Four Records
www.brecherjazz.com

Cma7 B♭ma6 Ami9
Chordal Inst ad lib. . . . .
21
day is young, each mo - ment is brand new. Won't be a
C
25
Dmi7 Cmi9 Dmi9
sad drag, I got a glad bag, that I can reach in - to. When e - ver
29
Dmi7 Cmi9 F♯mi7
day's woes be come the night's foe, I got a trick, or two to
33
Fma9 Emi7(♭5)/B♭ Fma7 Dmi6
help me re - mind my - self that time goes swift - ly by. Cher - ish the
37
Cma9 B♭ma9(♯11) Ami9
past, but have a blast, here and now.
39
Ami9 B♭ma9(♯11) A♭ma9 Fma9 E♭ma9 Dma7(♭5)

Solos:
Gmi9
Fmi7/G
Gmi9
Fmi9
Bmi9
Bmi7(11)
Dmi9
Cmi9
A♭ma9(♯11)
G♭ma9(♭5)
Fma7
E♭ma6
Dmi9
Gmi9
Fmi7/G
Gmi9
Gmi9
Fmi9
Bmi9
Bmi7(11)
B♭ma9/D
Ami7(♭5)/E♭
B♭maj6
Gmin6
Fma9
E♭ma7
Ami7(♭5)/E♭
Dmi9
Dmi11
(..won't be a.....)
after solos D.S. al Coda
Dmi6
Cma9
B♭ma9
Emi7(♭5)/B♭
by. Don't waste a bit, 'cause this is it. Go have some fun, be fore it's
Ami9
Cma9
B♭ma9(♯11)
Ami9
done. Cher - ish the past, but have a blast, here and now
Ami9
B♭ma9(♯11)
Ami9
here and now
B♭ma9(♯11)
Ami9
On Cue
Ami9
here and now
now!

Green

Ballad

Doug Drewes

Recorded on: The Drewes Brothers "The Drewes Brothers"/2013
www.drewesbrothers.bandcamp.com | www.dougdrewes.com

Hanauma Bay

Robert Campbell

www.musician.allaboutjazz.com/robertcampbell

Hand Me Down

Chris Aschman

He Walks among Us

for Cedric Napoleon

Jay Fluellen

Recorded on: Doc Gibbs and Picante "Servin' It Up Hot"

Hole in the Wall

Georgie Bonds

additional lyrics:

Long days and cold nights,
the long winter nights
Tryin' to find where I'm destined,
tryin' to do what seems right.
With the wind at my side, my horse
I'm astride.
Give me a sign, give me a sign

So far and so long
I've searched and I've tried
Lord knows I've tried to find others just like us
I'm talkin' about both of our kind
Those who would ride
(to coda)

Recorded on: Georgie Bonds "Sometimes I Wonder"
www.georgiebonds.com

Recorded on: The Dukes of Destiny "Higher"
www.arlynwolters.com

B
Cmi G7 Cmi
For lack of a bet-ter world I call it lo ve And there
Fmi G7 Cmi Fmi
is-n't a cure it ain't all sweets and ro - ses it's a sick-ness and it's a sin
Fmi Cmi Fmi Cmi Cmi G7
I call it love I call it love I call it lo-ve oh yeah
[voc. ad lib into solo]
C
Solos
Cmi
1. 2. 3.
A♭7 G7
4.
Cmi Fmi
What makes me tear out my hair, then it
Cmi Fmi Cmi
tears out my heart? What makes me tear my clothes in back of his car-
Cmi Fmi Cmi
what sells all the dia- monds, and the Val-en-tine cards? What-
Dmi7 D♭ma7 Cmi
D.S. al Coda
e-ver you call - it, that's you! But I call it lo ve! For
Solos Cmi G7
Cue next
Cmi G7
Could on-ly be
N.C.
Cmi
fine
lo - - - - - - ve!

Recorded on: Deb Callahan "Tell It Like It Is"
www.debcallahanband.com

D7(#9)
oh I got it good you know I got it bad for the things that you do
D7(#9)
// Solo break
D
D7(#9)
when you love me so good
D7(#9)
// [vocal break]
You got me mel ting a way
E
G7
D7(#9)
mm like but ter in the pan I can't think of nothing el se
G7
A7
oh come on and be my man you know you leave me want
D7(#9)
ing more You're the one that I a dore in the morn ing late at night
D7(#9)
D.S. al Coda
ya make me feel right when you love me like you do
D7(#9)
oh I got it bad for the things that you do when you love me so good
D7(#9)
oh I got it bad for the things that you do when you love me so good

I Miss Home

Medium Bossa

Bill Jolly

Dbma7 Fmi11 Bbmi9 C+7 Fmi9 Fmi9

A

Fmi Dbma7 G(sus4) C7 Fmi

Dbma7 G(sus4) C7 Fmi Bbmi9

Eb11 Eb7(b9) Gb9/Ab Abma7 D+9 Dbma7 Fmi11 Bbmi9

C+7 Fmi9 1. Fmi9 2. Fmi9

B

Dbma7 C7/E

Fmi7 F+9/A Bbm9 Eb11 Abma7 D+9 Dbma7 C7/E

Fmi Bb13(b5) C+7 Fmi9 Fmi9

Recorded on: Grover Washington, Jr., "Next Exit"/Columbia Records

www.billjolly.com

Recorded on: Alex Posmontier Quartet "Coast to Coast"
www.alexposmontier.com

In Waves

www.mattdavisguitar.com

Inside Out

Pat Martino

Soulfully

Recorded on: Pat Martino "Undeniable"/High Note Records, 2011
www.patmartino.com

Final Ending

Turnaround

Inspired by Highest Reason

for Dave Burrell

David Dzubinski

Solos:

For Solos feel free to use any varation of Blues changes, Blues styles, or fragments of Blues forms and/or ideas either in whole or in fragmented parts as a way of exploring the themematic material presented in the head of the piece.

Interpretation

Medium Swing

Inwood

John David Simon

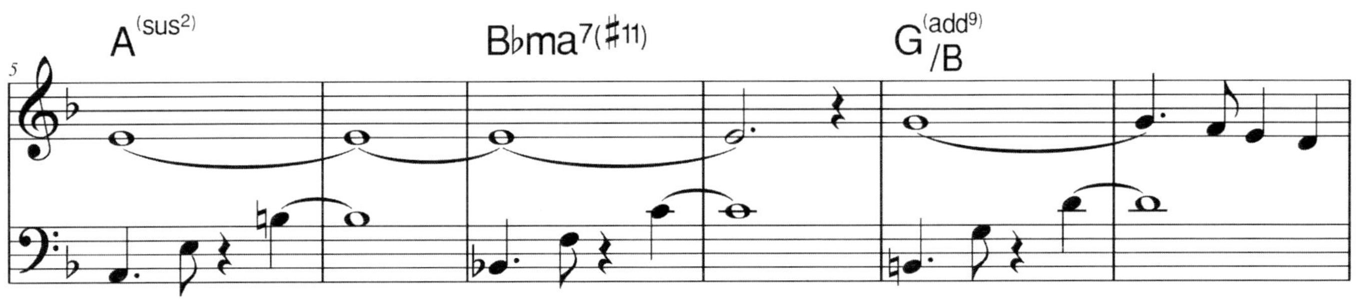

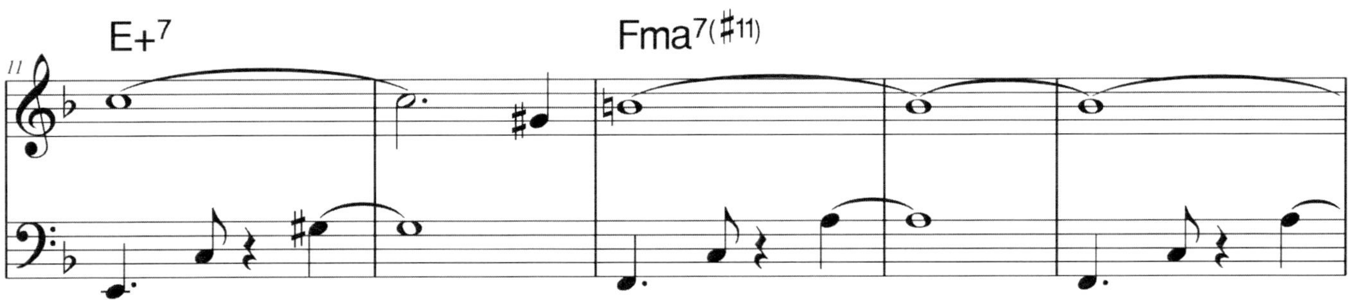

Recorded on: John David Simon "Phantasm"/WarmGroove Records, 2014
www.johndavidsimon.com

Cma13
Abma13
Fmi9/Bb
Fmi9/Bb
Ebma7/Bb
Fmi9/Bb
1st time only
Interlude [4x last time to Coda]
B
Ebma7/Bb
Fmi9/Bb
Ebma7/Bb
Fmi9/Bb
Play for D.S. only
last time ritard . . .
Solo form: A A B B
After solos D.S. al Coda
N.C.
Fma7(#11)
3

Is It Over My Head?

Larry McKenna

Lawrence McKenna Publishing/ASCAP
Recorded on: Larry McKenna "Profile"/Dreambox Media, 2009

Fmi7 Bb7 Eb G7(b9)
fine
To Solos
Solos
Cmi Dmi7(b5) G7(b9) Cmi Cmi7/Bb Ami7(b5) D7(b9)
Gmi Ami7(b5) D7(b9) Gmi7 Gb7
Fmi7 Bb7
1. Eb7
Ab9 Ab9 Cmi7(b5)
F7 B7 Bb7 G7(b9)
2.
Bbmi7 Bbmi7/Ab Gmi7(b5) C7 Fmi7 Abmi7 Db7
Eb Cmi7 F9 Fmi7 Bb7 Eb G7(b9)

Isla's Waltz

Christopher Marsceill

Recorded on: Reverend Chris "@etude"
www.plebo.org

It's Always There

Medium/Medium-up
Straight ♪s

Norman David

Jackson St.

Joseph Nocella

Recorded on: Ron Nocella "Urbanated"/1999
www.josephnocella.com

Jazz-o-etry to Complete Communion

Elliott Levin
6/2/17 NYC

The poem (left column) can be read with the notes in unison with their assigned syllables-rhythm to be agreed/felt between the performers, or words can be vocalized, then performed musically, as a melody, phrasing the notes as you would the words. Word and note phrases can answer each other copying and/or embellishing each other's phrasing and articulation. Or all of the above. The piece can be performed straight down, then improvised as a whole structure, or phrases can be expanded upon individually, moving on to the next as a segment's statement is explored.

The In-Omni-Cess/pres-ent — A | D F♯ D♯ G | E C

Inevitability spent — F D B A♭ F E♭ F | F♯

sense of events lent — G | F♯ G F♮ | G♯

to grasping the elusive — F | C A♭ | F C E♭ D

brass/golden ring — B♭ | E♭ A♭ C♯

grass bolden-ed — B | E G (F♯)

Bring it on! Phat . . . — F A C♯ // > E♭

Platidinous attitudes . . . — A F♯ D♯ G E | F A♭ D

attuned and accrued	B – F♯ | – G – B – E
to the long (haul)	B – D – C♯ | – (C♮)
and the lat-i-tudes . . .	F♯ – G♯ | – A – G♮ – F♮
It takes to make it	C♯ – E | – D♯ – G♯ – G♮
to fix a brake	C – G♯ | – E – C♯
to tell . . . a vision	D♯ – E | – A – E – C♯
of the shape of all that	D B – C♯ – A – E – A
Jazz . . . to come.	E♭ | – D – A

Joe's Delight

[Interlude]
D
Ebma7
Abmi7
Db7 Abmi7
Db7
Gbma7 Gb6 Gbma7
Drums: to sticks
f
with rhythm section
mf
decresc.
Gb6
F7
F7 Bb7
melody break
Eb6
melody break
p
cresc.
f
E
Solos
Fmi7 Bb7 Fmi7 Bb7 Fmi7 Bb7 Fmi7 Bb7(b9) Bbmi7 (Eb7)
Cmi7 (F7)
1.
Fmi7 Bb7 Ebma7
2.
Fmi7 Bb7 Ebma7
Bbmi7 Eb7 Abma7 Cmi7 F7
Fmi7 Bb7 Fmi7 Bb7 Fmi7 Bb7 Fmi7 Bb7
Fmi7 Bb7(b9) Bbmi7 (Eb7) Cmi7 (F7) Fmi7 Bb7 Ebma7
After Solos D.S. al Coda
Fmi7 Bb7
3
Ebma9
fine
p
3

Josephine

Medium Tempo

Music & Lyrics
"Father" John D'Amico

Recorded on: John D'Amico "Street Blues"/Dreambox Media, 1999 (1988 EARS-1010)

Fmi9 Eb7(sus4)
our___ hearts__ will find___ their__ true home.______
Abmi7(9) Db13 Abmi7(9) Db13
Don't___ be a - fraid to be free,______
F#mi7(9) B13 F#mi7(9) B13
dreams___ we hold dear can come true,______
Emi7(9) A13 Emi7(9) A13 Eb7(sus4)
when___ we be - lieve deep in - side.______
Eb7(sus4) Eb7 Ab Bb/Ab
Stars___ do___ shine___ Jo - se -
Ab Bb/Ab Ab Bb/Ab
phine______ Win - ter's___ a sigh___ be - fore
Ab Bb/Ab Fmi7(9)
spring.______ Life's___ ma - gic ne - - ver
Eb7(sus4) Fmi7(9) Eb7(sus4)
Vamp and fade Intro to End
dies.______ It's______ with in___ Jo - se - phine.

The Journey

Moderate
Freddie Paulin
♩=120
Intro C7(sus4) B♭mi7 C7(sus4) B♭mi7 C7(sus4) B♭mi7
8 B♭mi7 C7(sus4) B♭mi7 B♭mi7 A♭ma7
14 Ami7 D7 Gma7 A♭mi7 D♭7 G♭ma7
19 G♭ma7 F7(sus4)
25 A♭(sus4) B7(sus4)
30 B7(sus4) D7(sus4)
36 D7(sus4) C7(sus4) B♭mi7 B♭mi7
41 C7(sus4) B♭mi7 A♭ma7
46 Ami D7 Gma7 A♭mi7 D♭7 G♭ma7

Just Remembered

Ballad
Straight eighths

Sandy Eldred

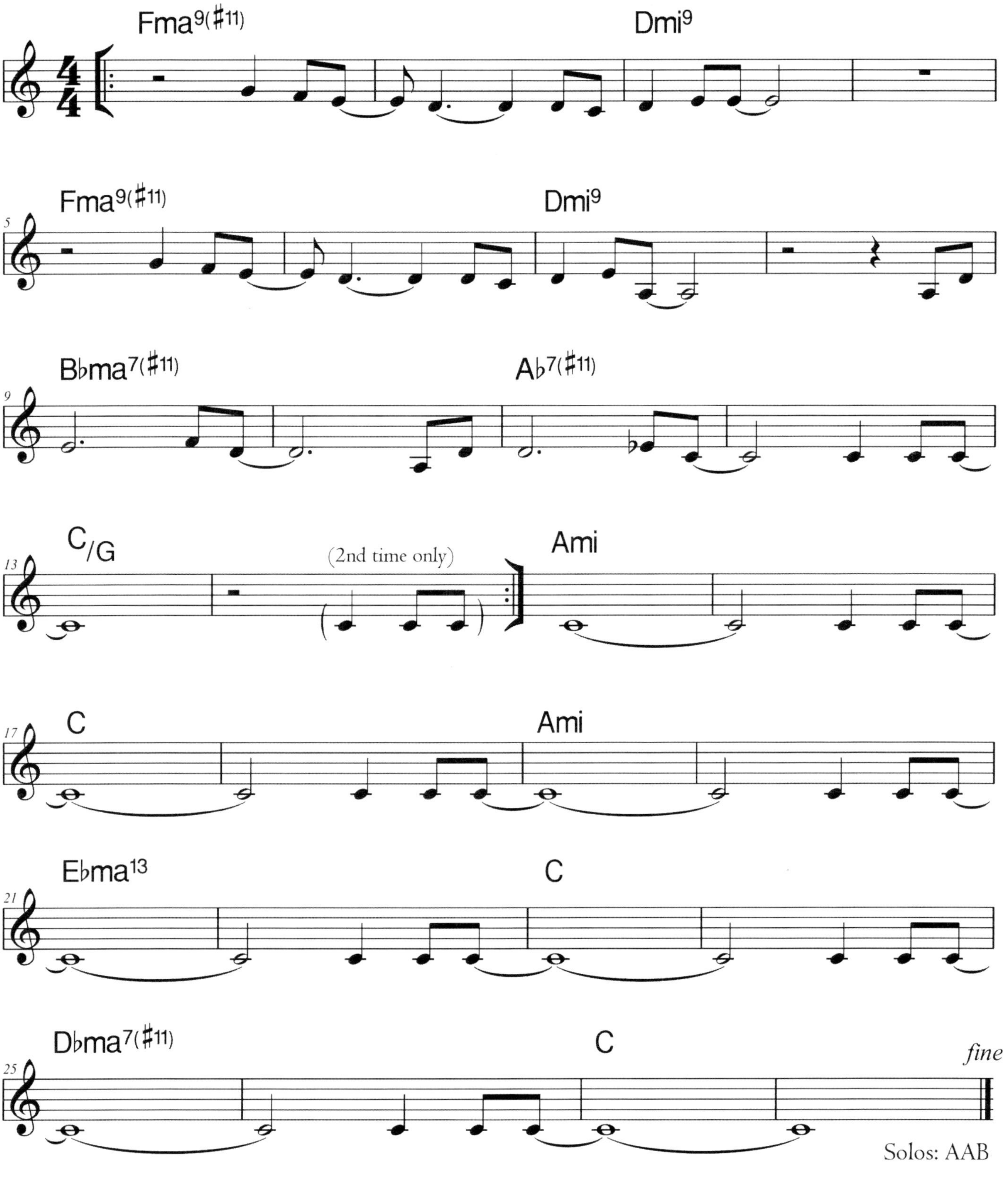
Fma9(♯11)
Dmi9
5
Fma9(♯11)
Dmi9
9
B♭ma7(♯11)
A♭7(♯11)
13
C/G
(2nd time only)
Ami
17
C
Ami
21
E♭ma13
C
25
D♭ma7(♯11)
C
fine
Solos: AAB

Juste un Peu de Chance

(With a Little Luck)

Music by Tom Glenn
Lyrics by Suzanne Cloud

Dmi7 G7 Cma7 Ebmi11
my love at a par - ty
D7(b5) Dbma7 Db6 Fmi7
in the sub - way ev - 'ry lit - tle corn - er shop I try to
Bb9 Cmi7 Bm7 Bbmi7 C7 C Fmi7
spy a glance from you, juste un peu de chance
Eo7 Go7 Abma7 F7 Bbmi7 Eb7
says I'm sure, you'll bump in - to me, out of the
C+7 B13 B9(b5) Bbmi11 Dbmi6
blue so have you been de - pend - ing on
Bbmi11 Eb13 Ab Gmi7(b5) C7
just a tin - y bit of luck too?
a hap - py phe - nom - en - non?
D.S. al Coda
Bmi11 E13 Bbmi11
Hop - ing to come up - on Just a
Eb9 Abma7 Bbmi7/Db 3x Abma7
lit - tle luck too.

Recorded on: "Tunnel Vision"/Reverie
www.dreamboxmedia.com

Dma7(add13)/E
Bass pedal E
E7(6/9)
A(add9)
A(add9)
vamp with drum fills
3X
Last time coda to
piano 8vb with bass/ N.C.
C
Solos
Dma7(13 9)
E/Dma7
Ama7
G/A
Dma7
Dma7
C♯mi7
Bmi7(11 9)
C♯7
F♯mi7
B7(9)
Dma7(add13)/E
Dma7(add13)/E
Dma7(add13)/E
A(add9)
B/A
D/A
A(add9)
After solos D.S. al Coda
A(add9)
fine
[suggested drum pattern on opening vamp]
Katy's Song - 2

Recorded on: Mike Boone Quartet "Beneath the Surface"/Truth Revolution Records

Solos
Swing
48
Dmi7 G7 Cmi7 F7 B♭mi7 E♭7(♭9) A♭ma7 D♭7(♯11)
56
C B♭/C C B♭/C F E♭/F F E♭/F D/E
64
D♭/E♭ E♭7(♯11) E♭/F F7(♯11) G♭/A♭ A♭7(♯11) G♭/A♭ A♭7(♯11)
After solos D.S. al Coda
Afro-Cuban
2/3 Rumba clave
Open Drum Solo
72
D♭ma7 G♭/A♭ D♭ma7 G♭/A♭
Drum solo
76
D♭ B/D♭ D♭ B/D♭ G♭ E/G♭ G♭ E/G♭
3x
84
D♭ B/D♭ D♭ B/D♭ G♭
[Drum solo Ends]
Swing
89
E/G♭ G♭ E/G♭ D/E D♭/E♭ E♭7(♯11)
94
E♭/F F7(♯11) G♭/A♭ A♭7(♯11) G♭/A♭
99
G♭/A♭ Dmi7 G7 Cmi7
103
F7 B♭mi7 E♭7(♭9) A♭ma7 D♭7(♯11)
107
D♭7(♯11) D♭7(♯11) D♭7(♯11) D♭7(♯11) D♭7(♯11) D♭7(♯11)
fine

Keno

Cha Cha

Byard Lancaster

Recorded on: Byard Lancaster - Keno Speller "Exactement"/Palm Records, 1974
www.ooopz.com/byard/

La Bahia Fosforecente

(The Bioluminescent Bay)

Latin Feel Ballad

Suzzette Ortiz

Recorded on: Suzzette Ortiz "Renacer"/2012

www.suzzetteortiz.com

Dmi
A(add2)
C(add2)
G(add2)
A(add2)
B(sus4)
E(sus4)
Last time D.S. al Coda
Ami7
Fma7
B°
E13
Solos
C
Ami
Fma9
Ami
Fma9
Ami
Fma9
B°
E7
Ami
D7
During Solos.
End of last Solo go to § at B
Dmi9
Emi7
Fma9
G
A
E13
A
Dmi9
Emi7
Fma9
G
Dmi9
Emi7
Fma9
G
A
fine
rit . . .

Lean Years

Recorded on: Pat Martino "Strings"/Prestige Records
www.patmartino.com

D♭mi9
Emi9
Gmi9
Emi9
D♭mi9
G♭13
C
Dmi9
E♭9
Dmi9
E♭9
Dmi9
E♭9
Dmi9
E♭9
Cmi9
F7(♭9)
B♭ma9
A7(♭13)
After solos: head out take Coda
Dmi9
E♭9
Dmi9
E♭9
Dmi9
E♭9
Dmi9
E♭9
To Solos
Final Ending
A7(♭13)
G13

Lemar Shongo

Monnette Sudler

Recorded on: Monnette Sudler "Let the Rhythm Take You"/MSM-Phillyinde
www.monnettesudlermusic.com

Let It Be Yesterday

Music & Lyrics by Ella Gahnt
Lyrics by Leon Mitchell

Recorded on: Ella Gahnt "Third Stage of Elegance"
www.ellagahnt.com

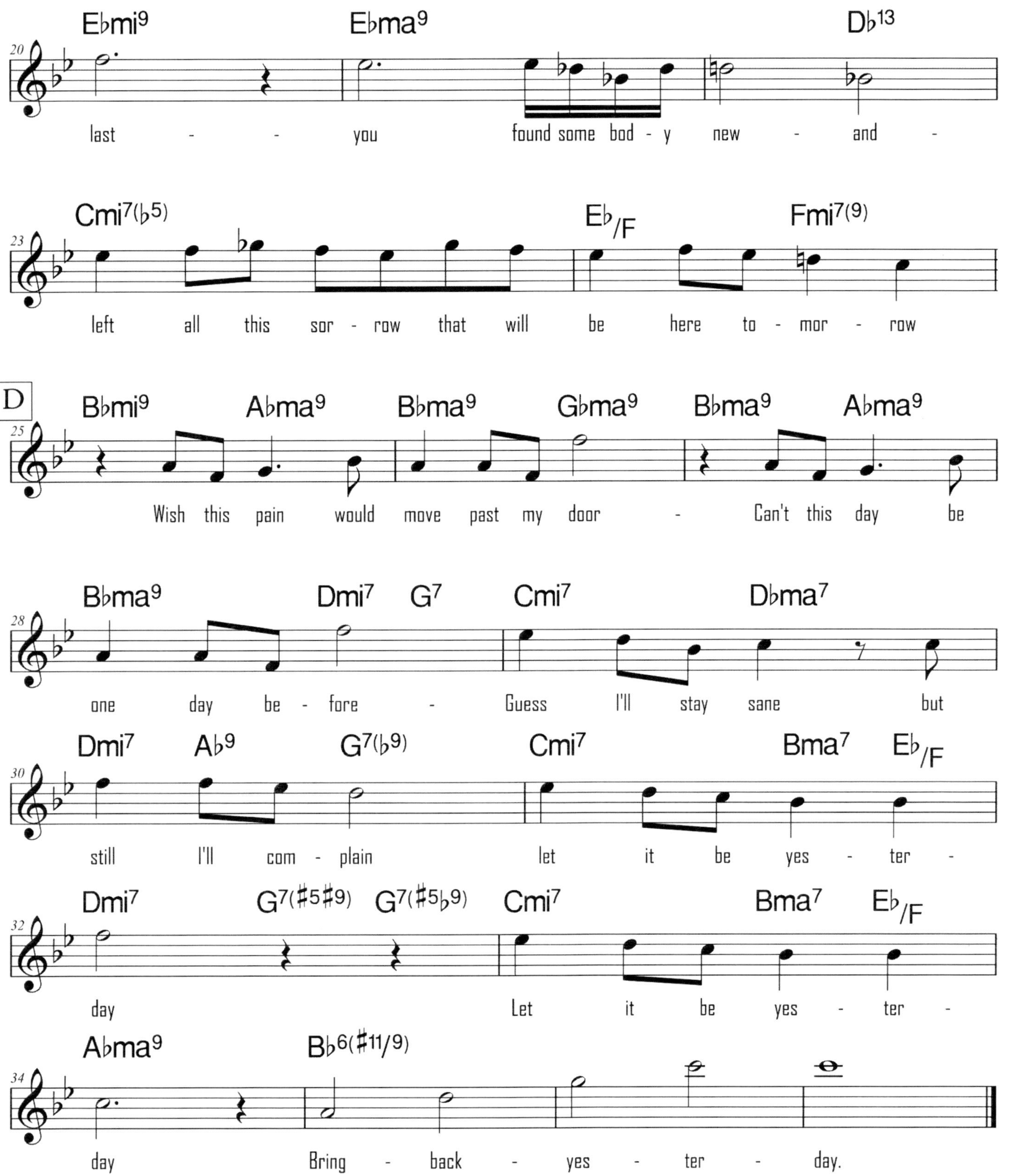

Ebmi9 Ebma9 Db13
last - - you found some bod - y new - and -
Cmi7(b5) Eb/F Fmi7(9)
left all this sor - row that will be here to - mor - row
D
Bbmi9 Abma9 Bbma9 Gbma9 Bbma9 Abma9
Wish this pain would move past my door - Can't this day be
Bbma9 Dmi7 G7 Cmi7 Dbma7
one day be - fore - Guess I'll stay sane but
Dmi7 Ab9 G7(b9) Cmi7 Bma7 Eb/F
still I'll com - plain let it be yes - ter -
Dmi7 G7(#5#9) G7(#5b9) Cmi7 Bma7 Eb/F
day Let it be yes - ter -
Abma9 Bb6(#11/9)
day Bring - back - yes - ter - day.

Let It Flow

for Dr. J

Grover Washington, Jr.

2.
D9
E♭ma7
Emi9(addA)
C
A9
Dmi9
Co7
Gmi7
Ami9
Ami9
A7+(♭9)
Dmi9
Gmi7
Ami9
A7+(♭9)
Dmi9
[Solos]
Dmi
Last time use pick up, D.S. (take 2nd ending) al Coda
(last time)
Gmi7
Repeat and fade

Let Me Cook for You

Music & Lyrics
Andrea Carlson

Recorded on: Andrea Carlson and Love Police "Love Can Be So Nice"/2016
www.andreacarlsonmusic.com

Additional lyrics:

There's no tellin' what's that stuff
But it's on your plate, so eat it up.
I just cooked this dish for you,
so hurry up and start to chew.
I can do all this for you, and maybe more
Oh honey, let me cook for you!
I'll whip you up some creamy mashed potatoes,
cornbread and some bright green fried tomatoes,
roasted chicken -lemon with rosemary
I'll end it with a cobbler of blueberry!
I can do all this for you, and maybe more

Recorded on: Dan Graper "Lighter than Air"/2017
www.dangrapermusic.com

First recorded on: "Swingin' with Roy Haynes"/Metronome MEP90

Little Man

Recorded on: Art Blakey and the Jazz Messengers "Album of the Year"/Timeless SJP 155

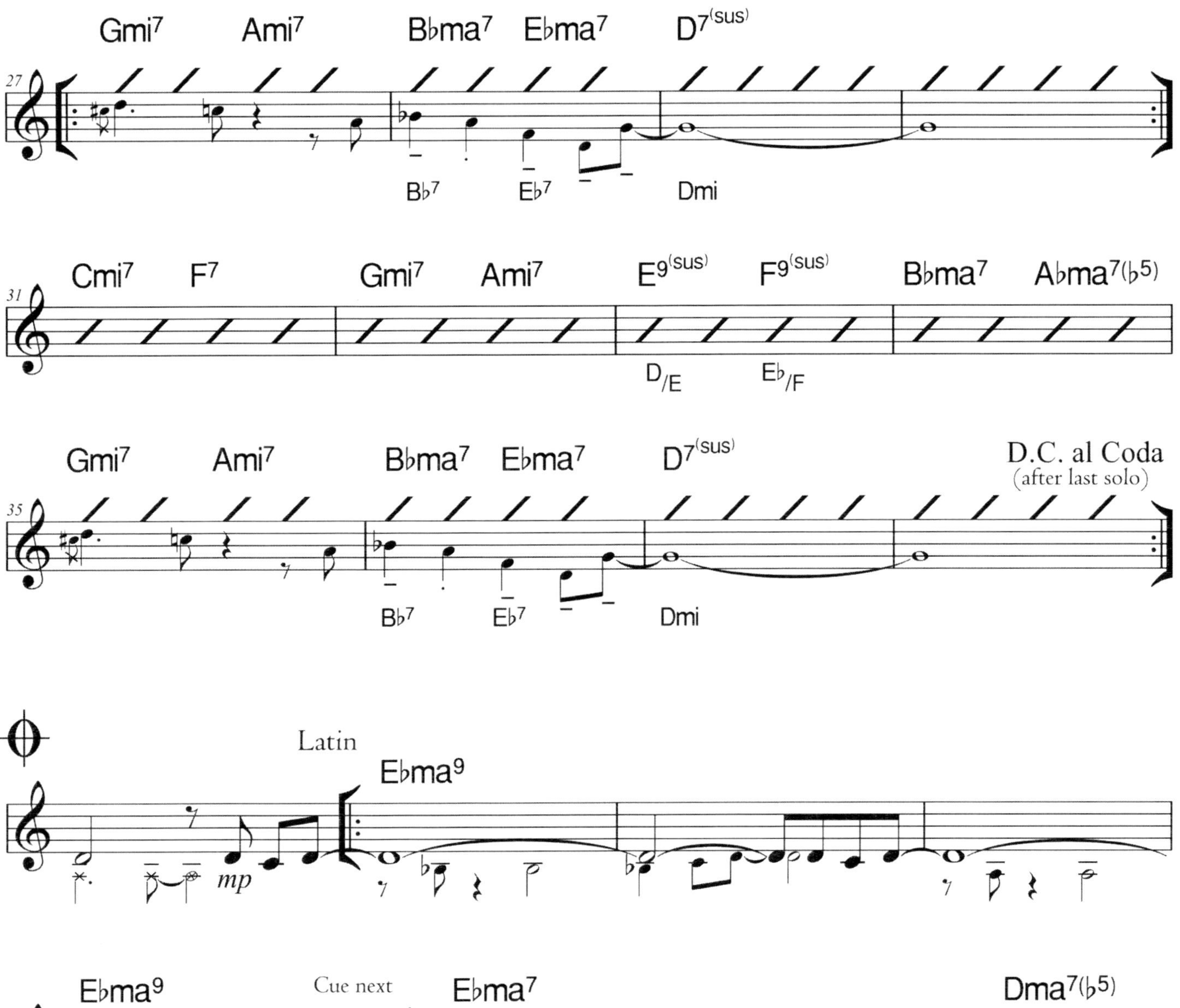
Gmi7 Ami7 Bbma7 Ebma7 D7(sus)
27
Bb7 Eb7 Dmi
Cmi7 F7 Gmi7 Ami7 E9(sus) F9(sus) Bbma7 Abma7(b5)
31
D/E Eb/F
Gmi7 Ami7 Bbma7 Ebma7 D7(sus)
D.C. al Coda
(after last solo)
35
Bb7 Eb7 Dmi
Latin
Ebma9
mp
Ebma9
Cue next
Ebma7
Dma7(b5)
rit.

Little Miss Lady

Edward "Eddie" Green
Morris "Mo" Bailey

Recorded on: Catalyst "Unity"/Muse Records

Dmi
Lit - tle la - dy play - ing grown up games
Dmi
mother's helpers getting in the way
Dmi B7(♯9) E7(♯9) A7(♯9)
Rag - ge - dy Ann can spend the
D7(♯9) E♭mi9/A♭
night with you No I don't know how long dad - dy will be gone
E♭mi9/A♭ Emi9/A
I'm here be
Emi9/A
side you lit - tle Miss la - dy
Dmi Dmi6 Dmi7 Dmi Dmi
Now it's time to rest your
Dmi7 B♭/D Dmi
wea - ry head
D.S. to

Loony Blues

Music by John Swana
Lyrics by Wendy Simon

Recorded on: Mike Boone "Heart and Soul"/Dreambox Media, 2014
https://musicians.allaboutjazz.com/johnswana

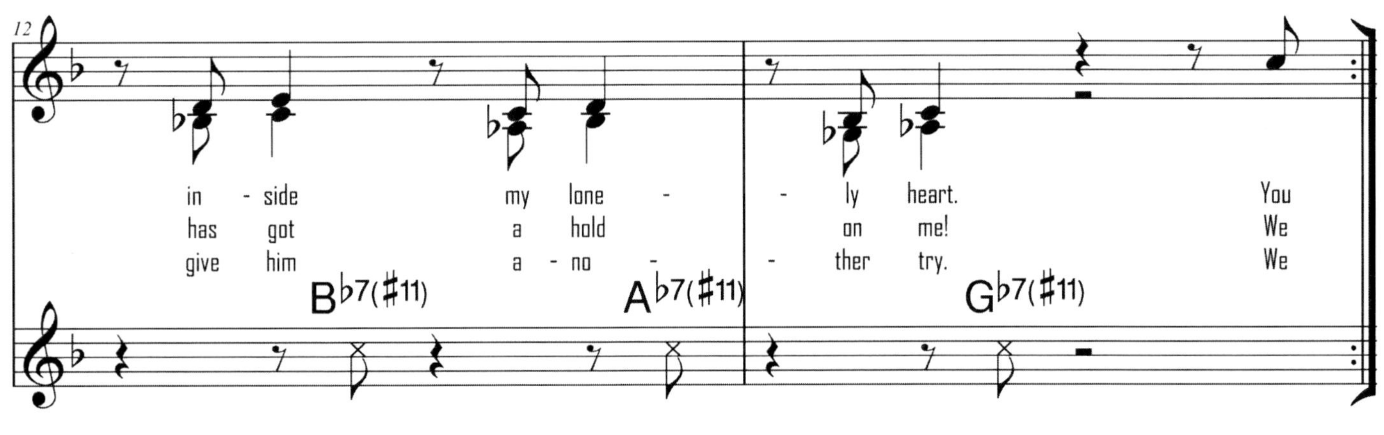
12
in - side my lone - - ly heart. You
has got a hold on me! We
give him a - no - - ther try. We
B♭7(♯11)
A♭7(♯11)
G♭7(♯11)

14
feel the way I do. We'll work it out,
see. I'll let it be. The loon - y blues
A♭7(♯11)
G♭7(♯11)
E7(♯11)
C7(♯11)

fine
16
this time, just me and you. It's plain to
has got a hold on me. It's Lo ony!
B♭7(♯11)
A♭7(♯11)
G♭7(♯11)
F7

Love Is to Blame

Keli Vale & Nick Bucci

© Keli Vale & Nick Bucci
Recorded on: Keli Vale & Nick Bucci "Sweetness"
www.kvnbmusic.com

G F♯7 F7 E7
Ev - 'ry - thing's al - right soon as I hear you coo Your
Ami11 D6 G D.S. al Coda
love wash - es my trou - bles a - way.
G♯(sus4) C♯7 A
diz zy Your voice is turn - ing to
G♯7 G7 F♯7 Bmi11
my fa - vor - ite sound, and I sus - pect that
E6 C♯mi7(♭5) F♯7 Bmi7
love is to blame; yes, I know that
E6 A
love is to blame.

Lovelife

Joe Straczynski

A Lullaby, Dear Monk

Music by Jef Lee Johnson
Lyrics by Suzanne Cloud

Ballad

Recorded on: Suzanne Cloud "With a Little Help from My Friends"/Dreambox Media
www.dreamboxmedia.com

15
Bbmi7
Eb7(b9)
Slow
eff er ve scent touches here and there

17
Abma9
Db7/Ab
Abma7
G7(#5)
bend ing space time and pl ace can you hear reflect

19
Cmi7
F7
Eb7 Ab7 Db7 Gb7 G7 C7
ions in th e tune? Oh wait a minute now he's say ing

C
21
F7(b5)
Eb7(b5)
G7
Abma6
Close your eyes Re al ize Where the mo ment flies to.

25
D7(#9) G7(#5)
C7/G Gb7(#5)
Fmi7 Bb7
Gmi7 C7(b9)
Can't you see what this music means to me? I con cen trate my love on you

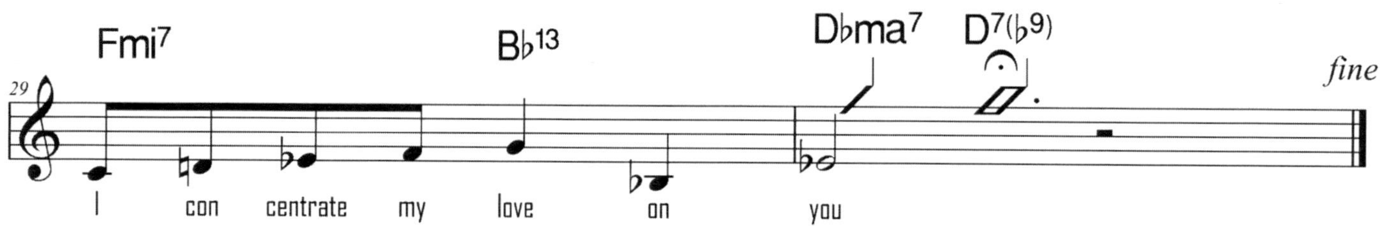
29
Fmi7
Bb13
Dbma7 D7(b9)
fine
I con centrate my love on you

Mandela

John Blake, Jr.

Recorded on: John Blake, Jr. "Adventures of the Heart"/Gramavision 18-8705-1

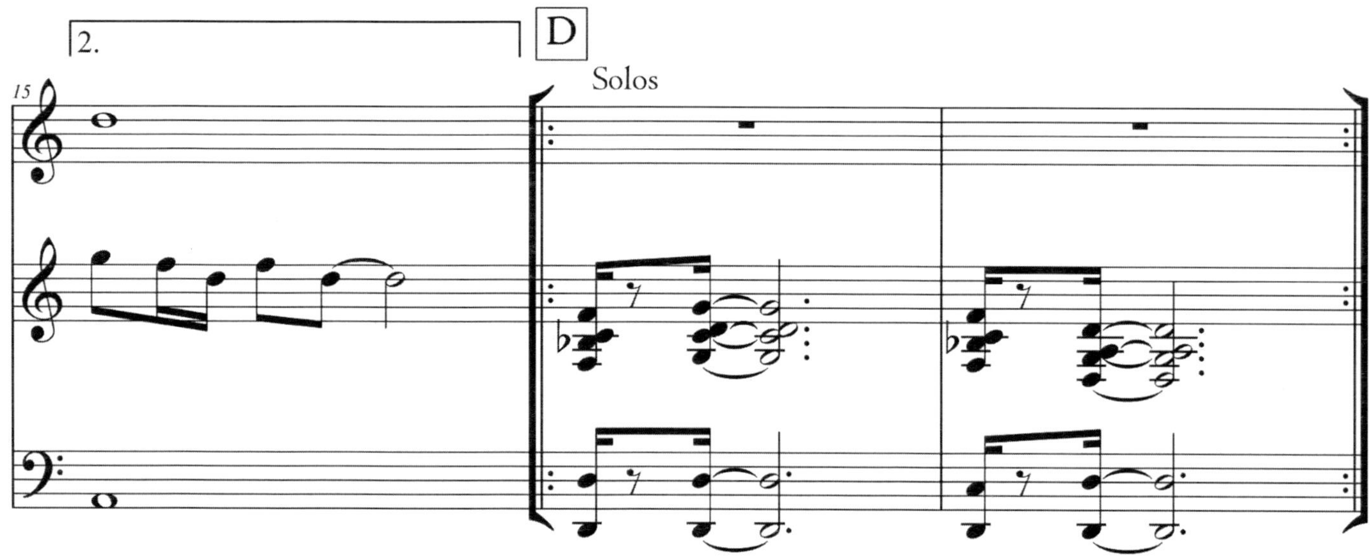

Form: Intro A B A B C B D C B A

Margie Pargie

(AM Rag)

Dave Burrell

Recorded on: Dave Burrell "High Won-High Two"/Arista Freedom, 1976

www.daveburrell.com

Matt's Blues

A Twisted Tail

Emile D'Amico

Blues

Recorded on: Don Glanden "Only Believe"/Cadence Jazz Records, 1999

www.donglanden.com

Miles Away

Slow with a bit of funk

Alan Lewine

Form: Head- A, B, Tag, C, C
Solos- A, B, C, C
Head out- A. B. Tag.

Mingus Mood

Slow with triplet feel

Sumi Tonooka

Recorded on: Sumi Tonooka and Erica Lindsay "Initiation"/Artists Recording Collective, 2009

Recorded on: Eric Mintel Quartet "Ground Breaker"
www.ericmintelquartet.com

Mother Tree

Kelly Meashey &
Randy Sarles

Recorded on: "The Inner Urge"/Dreambox Media
www.kellymeashey.com | www.dreamboxmedia.com

1.
Ami9(♯5)
2. Ami9(♯5)
C
Dmi9 Emi9 Ami9
With arms out stretched and reach ing up ward to the sun I take my place
Dmi9 Emi9 Am9
I stand be side you and can wea - ther an - y storm that comes my way
Dmi13 Emi9 Fma9(add13) F/G
Ge ner - a - tions pass and you stand
Ami(add2) Ami(add2)/G Ami(add2)/F Ami(add2)/E
strong
Ami(add2) Ami(add2)/G Ami(add2)/F Ami(add2)/E
D
Ama9 Bmi11/A Dmi9 Cma9 B♭ma7(♯11)
solo vamp
2nd time D.S.al Coda
Ami(add2) Ami(add2)/G Ami(add2)/F Ami(add2)/E
E7(♯9) Ami(add2) Ami(add2)/G Ami(add2)/F Ami(add2)/E
fine
For all

Mr. AA

Recorded on: Byard Lancaster "It's Not up to Us"/Rino-Atlantic/Vortex/Water Music Records

My Kind of Blues

Music by Lee Smith
Lyrics by Wendy Simon

Blues

Recorded on: Lee Smith "My Kind of Blues"/Vectordisc, 2015
www.leesmithmusic.com

Shuffle feel

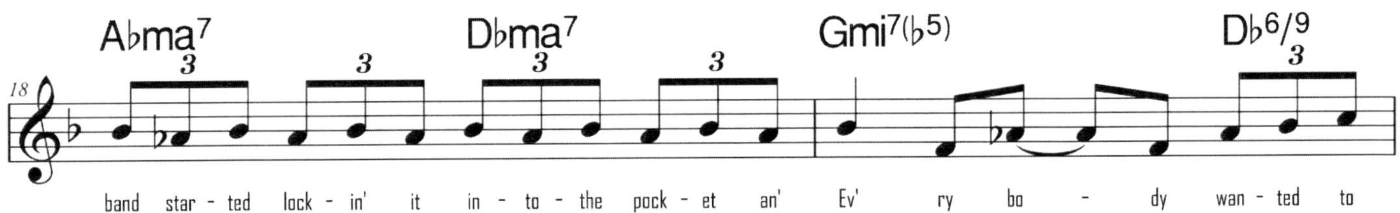

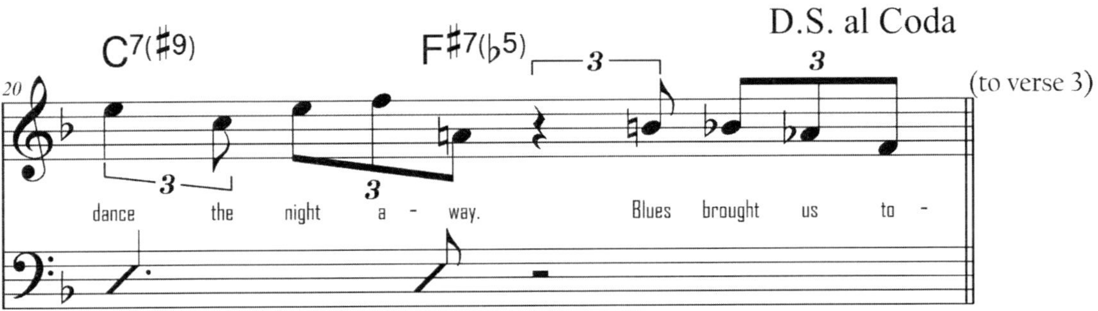

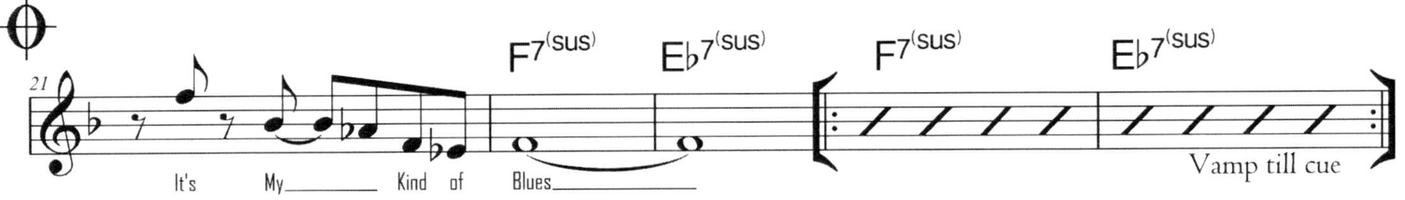

-Additional Lyrics -

Verse 2:

The Waiter came over, and brought my glass of wine
Some folks sat beside me, we hit it off just fine.
We all dug the music, and got into the groove,
Our bodies were shakin', so we got up to move.
Each one of us knew it, It's My Kind of Blues!

Verse 3:

Blues brought us together, it really felt so right.
The music was swingin', strangers were friends tonight,
Not all blues are sad ones, some can be happy too,
We all said let's make this, a weekly thing to do.
'Cause everyone felt it, It's My Kind of Blues!

My Love

Lyrics by Cathy Rocco
Music by Cathy Rocco & George Mesterhazy

Swing

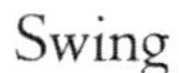

Dbma7 C7(b9) Fmi7 Bb13 Bbmi7 Eb7
knew some day you'd come to be my one and on - ly one My Love
C
Ab C+7 F+7(b9) Bbmi7 Gmi7(b5) C7(#9)
I feel so a - live and free to - get - her for- ev - er we'll
Fmi7 Bb7(sus4) Bb13 Ebmi9 Ab13
be just hold me oh so tight
D
Dbma7 Co Bbmi7 Eb7 Cmi7 Cmi7/F F7
my love__ my love my love my love we'll
Bb7 Eb7 Ab6/9 Bmi7 E7
Live eve - ry day as if it's the last my love
Solo
E
Ama7 C#+7 F#+7(b9) Bmi7 G#mi7(b5) C#7(#9) F#mi7 B7(sus4)
B13 E7(sus4) E7(b9) Ama7 C#+7 F#+7(b9) Bmi7
G#mi7(b5) C#7(#9) F#mi7 B7(sus4) B13 Emi9 A13
I've Wait ed

F
Dma7 C#o Bmi7 E7 C#mi7 Emi7 A7
so ve - ry long for you You've made my World brand new some how I
Dma7 C#7(b9) F#mi7 B13 Bmi7 E+7
knew some day you'd come to be my one and on - ly one My Love
G
Ama7 C#+7 F#+7(b9) Bmi7 G#mi7(b5) C#7(#9)
I feel so a - live and free to - get - her for - ev - er we'll
F#mi7 B7(sus4) B13(b9 b5) Emi9 A13
be just hold me oh so tight
H
Dma7 C#o Bmi7 E7 C#mi7 F#7(sus4) F#7(b9)
my love my love my love my love we'll
B7(sus4) B7 1.2. E7(sus4) E7(b9) A6 A13
Live eve - ry day as if it's the last my love
3. E7(sus4) E7(b9) Gma7 C6/9 Fma7
if it's the last my love
Fma7 Bbma7 A6/9

Mystery Blues

F Blues

Lucas Brown

The Next Time I See You

Bobby Zankel

Recorded on: Bobby Zankel Quintet "Prayer and Action"/CIMP Records and
Bobby Zankel Trio "Transcend and Triumph"/CIMP Records
www.bobbyzankel.net

F11(♭9)
no long fare wells
F11(♭9)
next time I see you I might just be you and you just might be me
E♭ma7(♭5)
D♭ma7(♭5)
Bma7
Bma7(♭5)

Ama7
Ama7(♭5)
D7+9
D7+9
C7+9
C7+9
D♭11
E11
D11
F11
E♭11
G♭11
G11(♭9)
G11(♭9)
G11(♭9)
G11(♭9)

Nightingale

Music by Lou Lanza
Lyrics by Joy Remetta

C
Bbmi7 Eb7 Abmi7 Db7 F#mi9 B9 Ema7 C#mi7
34
sing on in pain, of pain, for pain, sing of things that trou- ble me, and
F#mi7 B7 Ema7 F9(#11) Bb7(add13) Ami7 G7 F7 E7(b9)
38
peo - ple would stop to lis - ten to me. Sing to grace - ful - ly. And
D
Ami Ami/G# Ami/G Ami/F# Fma7 Bb7 Bmi7(b5) E7
42
as they's lis - ten to my song they would not see my pain. They
Abmi6 Db7 Gb Ebmi7 Gmi7(b5) C7(add13) Fma7
46
would not hear it, see it, feel it, for hap - pi - ness sounds the same. Oh
Emi7(b5) A Dma7 Gma7 C#mi7(b5) F#7 Bma7
50
night - ing - ale, of what do you sing? And are you lone - ly too? Do you
Bmi7 E9 A F#mi7 1. Bmi7(b5) E7 Ami
54
need some - one who you can love some - one to sing for you?
2. Bmi7(b5) E7(b9) A
58
one to sing for you?
*(Optional music for mm 34-37)
F#mi7 B7 Ema7 F9(#11) Emi7(b5) A7 Bmi7(b5) E7(b9)
60
Peo - ple would stop to lis - ten to me sing so grace - ful - ly. And

No Picnic

Music by Steve Giordano
Lyrics by Carla Jenkins
Eight Note Feel
♩=120
F♯mi9
Ami9/D
Bb(add9)
E7(♯11 ♯9)
Dma7
Fma7(b5)
Sum - mer em - bers burn to fan the flame of love
Ash - es in the dust will ne - ver be the same
Cmi9
Ema7
Emi9
Fmi9
B/Db
Beau - ty in the glow the wind be - gins to flow
Ama7
Eb9(♯11)
Gmi7
Bbmi7
you feel
I'm yours
for - e - ver more

No Room for Squares

Hank Mobley

Nommo

Jymie Merritt

Solos: vamp on A, play melody pickup to cue B

As transcribed by Greg Toro from Max Roach "The Drum Also Waltzes"/Atlantic Records, 1966

Recorded on: Shirley Scott "Oasis"/Muse Records, 1989
www.musicians.allaboutjazz.com/shirleyscott

Obsessive

Zoe Lowry

Recorded as single: Zoe Lowry "Obsessive"/Groove Control Recordings
www.zoelowry.com

Ok, Now What?

Jeff Baumeister

Recorded on: Jeff Baumeister "Pretty Melodies, for People Who Dig That Sort of Thing"

Old Bugs and New

Dave Posmontier

Recorded on: Dave Posmontier Quartet "Posterity"/Dreambox Media/Bands Not Bombs Publishing
www.daveposmontier.com

Solos
F7
Eb7
Bb7
Ab7
F7
Eb7
F7
D7(b9)
G7(#9 #5)
C7(#9)
F7
Eb7
[Interlude Between Solos]
Eb/F
Db/Eb
p
Db/Eb
Dmi7
1,2. . . . etc
After last solo D.S. al Coda
E/Gb
Gb/Ab
mf
C7
Db7
D7
Eb7
E7
f
C7
Db7
D7
f
[4x]
F7 Eb7
mp
f
fine

On the Midnight Special

Medium Slow Shuffle

Pat Martino

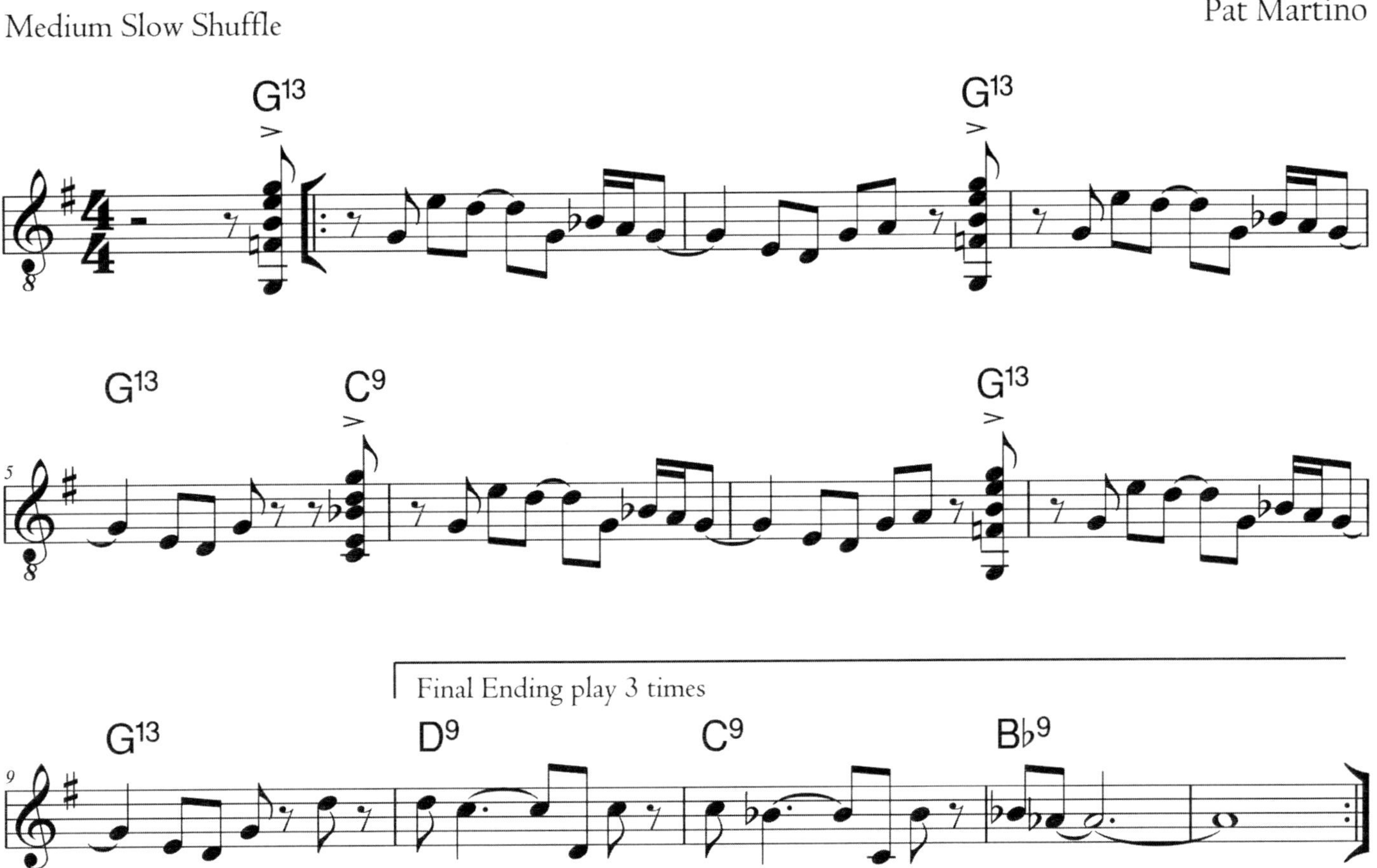

Recorded on: Pat Martino "Undeniable"/High Note Records, 2011
www.patmartino.com

One Falling Tree

Music by Larry McKenna
Lyrics by Melissa Gilstrap

Lawrence McKenna Publishing/ASCAP/Melissa Gilstrap Publishing/ASCAP
Recorded on: Larry McKenna "From All Sides"/2013
www.melissagilstrap.com

One for Sir Price

Jim Holton

Medium Swing

Recorded on: Jim Holton "No Green Bananas, a Retrospective"/Dreambox Media
www.jimholtonmusic.com

The One Who Heals

for Hannibal Lokumbe

Only the Moon and the Stars

Music & Lyrics
Patricia King Haddad

Recorded on: "Blue Azul"/1996
www.minasmusic.com

B
Ebmi9
Ab13(b9)
F#mi9
mf
May - be it's hea - ven - ly scheme
As I - close my eyes and can
B13
Ema7
Eb7(#9)
on - ly see - The mo - ments that we love with the strength from the stars high a -
Dma7
Ebmi9
Ab13(b9)
Ema7
- bove Or is our love in our hands
cresc.
To change what des - ti - ny in -
Ebmi9
Dma7
C#ma7
tends Or shape the course of its plans?
Solos
C#ma7
C
E∅7
Asus(b9)
Dma13
Ebma13
E∅7
Asus(b9)
Dma13
Ab7(b5)
Gma13
C9
Fma13
Bb9
E∅7
D.S. al Coda
Asus(b9)
Dma13
1.
2.
Dma13
D
C#ma7
E∅7
Asus(b9)
Dma7
Ebma7
Watch - ing the waves and the tide Is there
E∅7
Asus(b9)
Dma7
Ab7(b5)
Gma7
some thing in the moon or the stars that de - cide? How our love

C9 Fma7 Bb9 Eø7
will un - fold Is there some thing in the moon and the
Asus(b9) Dma7 Ab7(b5) Gma7 C9
stars that seem to - know? Is our love as true As this
Fma7 Bb9 Eø7
sky is blue? Is the ans - wer high a - bove or here - be -
Asus(b9) Abmi9 C#13(b9)
low? Would it ev - er re - veal ev - er show? -
Eø7 Asus(b9) Ebma13
On - ly the moon and the stars that seem to know
E
Ebma13(#11) Dma13
f On - ly the moon - and the stars seem to know
Ebma13(#11) Dma13
On - ly the moon - and the stars seem to know
Dma13 Ebma13 Dma13
On - ly the moon - and the stars seem to know
rit. . . . .

The Opener

Funky Shuffle Feel

Andy Lalasis &
John Mulhern

D
Solos
Fmi9
B♭13
4x
Dmi9
G13
4x
Fmi9
B♭13
3x
Fmi9
B♭13
B♭13 A13 A♭13
Dmi9
G13
Dmi9
Dmi9
G13
Dmi9
G13
Dmi9 G13
drum fill . . .
E
C6/9
B7(♯5)
B♭13
A7
Dmi9
G13
Dmi9
G13
C6/9
B7(♯5)
B♭13
A7
Dmi9
G13
Dmi9
G13
F
A♭ma7
A♭ma7
G11
A♭ma7
G11
G11
G
C6/9
B7(♯5)
B♭13
A7
Dmi9
G13
Dmi9
G13
Fmi9
B♭13
Fmi9
B♭13
Fmi9
B♭13
Fmi9
B♭13
Fmi9
B♭13
D♭13
fine

Opening Day

Music & Lyrics
Heath Allen

Bass on back beat
E♭mi7 F/E♭ E/E♭ E♭
Good - - bye safe life,
Bass walks
Emi9 A13 Dma7
I'm throw - in' cau - tion to the wind.
Bass on back beat
G♭mi7 A♭/G♭ G/G♭ G♭
Fare - - well sane life, it's
Bass walks
Fmi7 B♭7
time for the sea - son to be - gin.
E♭ G7 Cmi B♭mi7 E♭7
There will be some cloud y days some craz - y hops and rain de - lays,
A♭ D7+ Gmi7 C7
strike outs, put- outs, pick-offs and passed balls. You
Fmi7 A♭mi9 D♭13 Gmi7 C7
play the game, you take a chance, you may be lo-sers, may be champs. Like
F7 E7 E♭7 D7
rob - ins in the spring, I love it when they sing, "Let the
G7(♭9) C7 Fmi7 B♭7 E♭7(♯11)
game be - gin, play ball!"

Ortlieb's

John Swana

Medium Up Swing

Recorded on: John Swana and the Philadelphians "Philly Gumbo 2"
www.johnswana.com

Other Side of the Gemini

Recorded on: Hardly Records/Sister Carrying a Tradition Publishing/BMI
www.monnettesudlermusic.com

1.
2.
B♭ma7
B♭6/9 A7(♭9)
D
Solo I
Dmi9
B♭ma7
A+7(♭9)
This ending for solo
This ending out of solo
Dmi9
B♭ma7
1.
2.
B♭ma7
A7(♭9)
A♭ma7(♭5)
Drum fill . . .
E
Gmi7
Ami7
D7(♯9)
3x
Gmi7
Ami7
D7(♯9)
This ending for solo
This ending out of solo
Solo 2
Gmi7
Ami7
D7(♯9)
Ami7 D7(♯9)
D.S.al Coda
A♭ma7(♭5)
Drum fill . . .
A♭ma7(♭5)
fine
ff
cresc.

Our Yesterdays, Our Tomorrows

(A Song for Theo)

Recorded on: Kendrah E. Butler-Waters "Faith Walk"/BMI
www.kendrahbw.com

Pack 'n Roll

Medium Funk Samba

Recorded on: Steve Strawitz "Songs for Viola-Lin"/2004

B♭/C Bmi7(add11) B♭/C Bmi7 C/D B/D B♭ma7 Ami7 Gma7
fine
C
Ema7(♯11) E7(sus4) E6 E7(sus4)
F♯7(sus4)/E Ema7(♯11) E7(sus4) E6
F♯7(sus4)/E C7(sus4)/E
D
G♯mi7 F♯mi11
G♯mi7 Ami/B A/B
Solos
E
B♭ma7 Ami7 Dmi7 Emi7(♭5) A7
Dmi7 B♭ma7 Ami7 Dmi7 Em7(add9) B♭ma7
Ami7 Dmi7 Emi7(♭5) E♭7(add9) Dmi7
F
D♭ma7 Cmi7 Fmi7

C7(sus4) Bmi7(sus4) C7(sus4) Bmi7(sus4)
G
C7(sus4) Bmi7(sus4) C/D B/D
Bbma7 Ami7 G(add9)
H
B/C# F#/C# E(add9)
E(add9) B/C# F#/C# B/A
I
Bbma7 Ami7 G(add9)
B/C# F#/C# E(add9) B/C# F#/C# B7(sus4)
Cue next
J
Bbma7 Bmi7 F/C F/C#
Ebma7 Emi7(b5) F7(sus4)
To next solo at I
K
Ema7(#11) E7(sus4) E6 E7(sus4) F#7(sus4)/E
Ema7(#11) E7(sus4) E6
F#7(sus4)/E C7(sus4)/E
Cue next
D.S al fine

The Painter

Ari Hoenig

Recorded on: Ari Hoenig "The Painter"/Smalls Records, 2004

www.arihoenig.com

Dmi7 E♭ A♭ G♭
F(sus) B♭ Ami7(♭5) D7 Gmi7 F♯mi7 B♭(sus)
E A♭7(sus)
fine
C Solos
B♭ A♭/B♭ B♭ A♭/B♭ B♭ A♭/B♭
B♭ Ami7(♭5) D7 Gmi7 G♭(♯5)/A♭ Gmi7 A♭13
1. Gmi7 G♭(♯5)/A♭ Gmi7 Cmi7 F7
2. Gmi7 B♭/F Emi7(♭5) A7(♭5)
Dmi7 E♭ A♭ma7 G♭
Last time cue next
[Play Interlude* between solos]
F(sus)
D.C. al Fine
* Interlude
F(sus) B♭ Ami7(♭5) D7 Gmi7 F♯mi7 B♭(sus)
E A♭(sus)
To next solo at C

Paradise

John Blake, Jr.

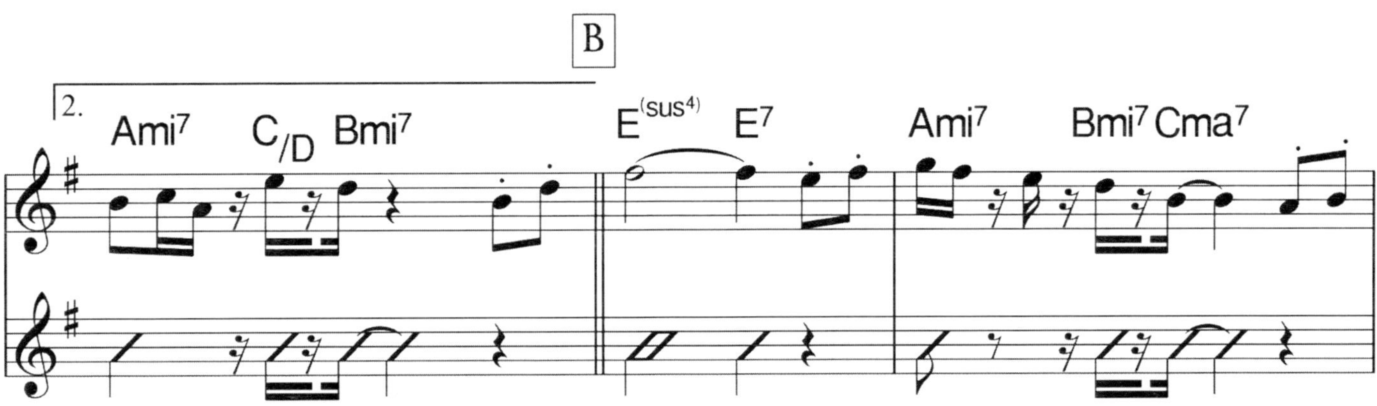

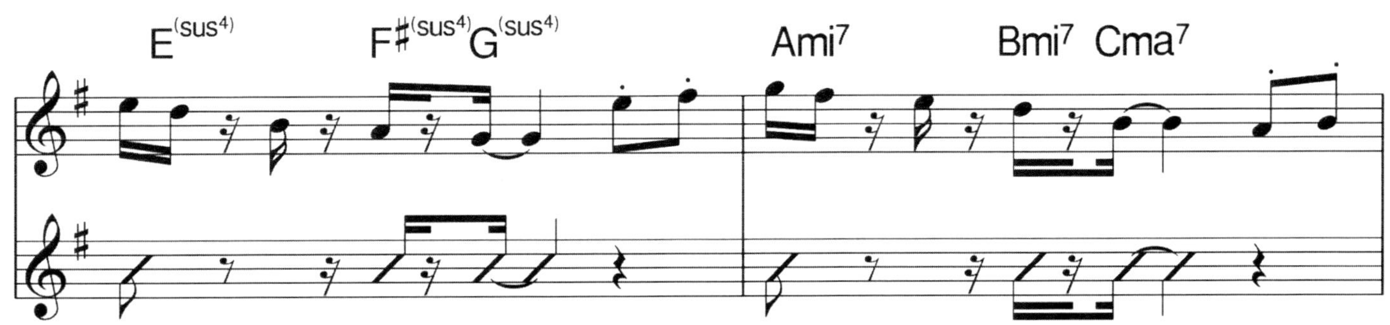

Recorded on: Grover Washington, Jr. "Paradise"

E(sus4)
F♯(sus4)
G(sus4)
Cma7
Bmi7
Ami7

Ami7
G
Ami7
Bmi7
Cma7
Bmi7
Ami7

Ami7
G
Ami7
Bmi7
Cma7
Bmi7
Ami7
G
Ami7
Bmi7
3

Cma7
Bmi7
C/D

Solos
Cma7
C/D
D/E
Ami7
C/D
Bmi7

Peace Bridge

Joey DeFrancesco

Recorded on: Joey DeFrancesco "Project Freedom"/Mack Avenue

www.joeydefrancesco.com

Pearl's Theme

Warren Oree

♩=Wherever you're at

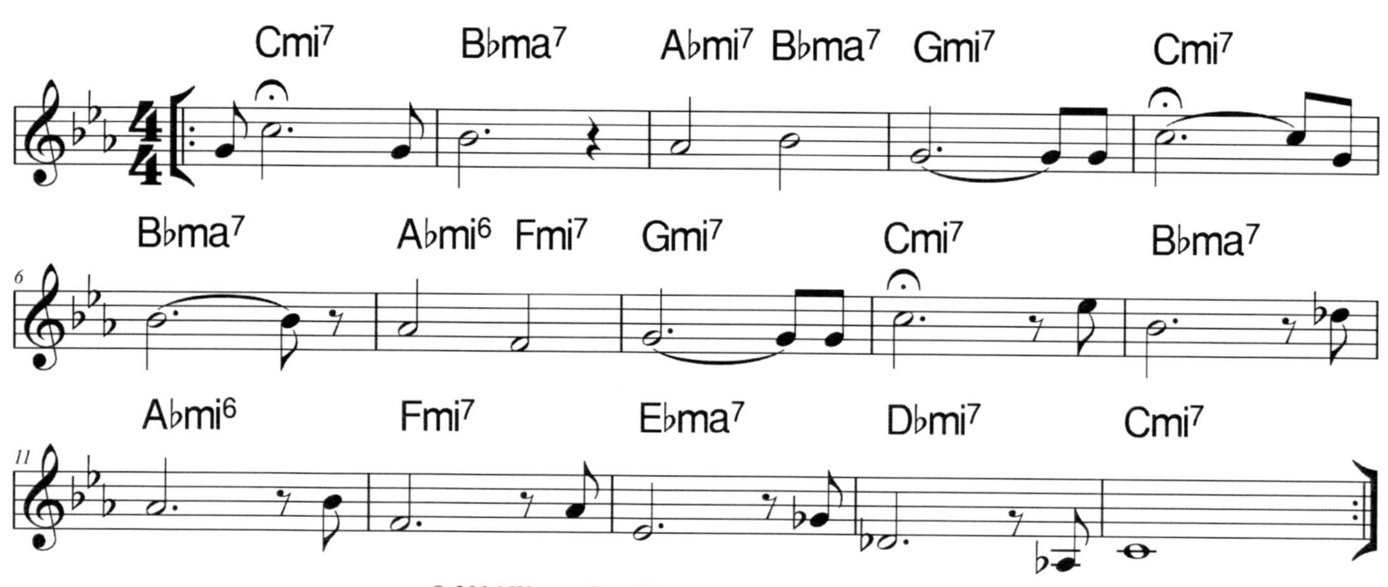

Cmi7
Bbma7
Abmi7 Bbma7 Gmi7
Cmi7
Bbma7
Abmi6 Fmi7
Gmi7
Cmi7
Bbma7
Abmi6
Fmi7
Ebma7
Dbmi7
Cmi7

Recorded on: Warren Oree & the Arpeggio Jazz Ensemble "Touching Bass"
www.arpeggiojazzensemble.com

Space City

♩=Wherever you're at

Warren Oree

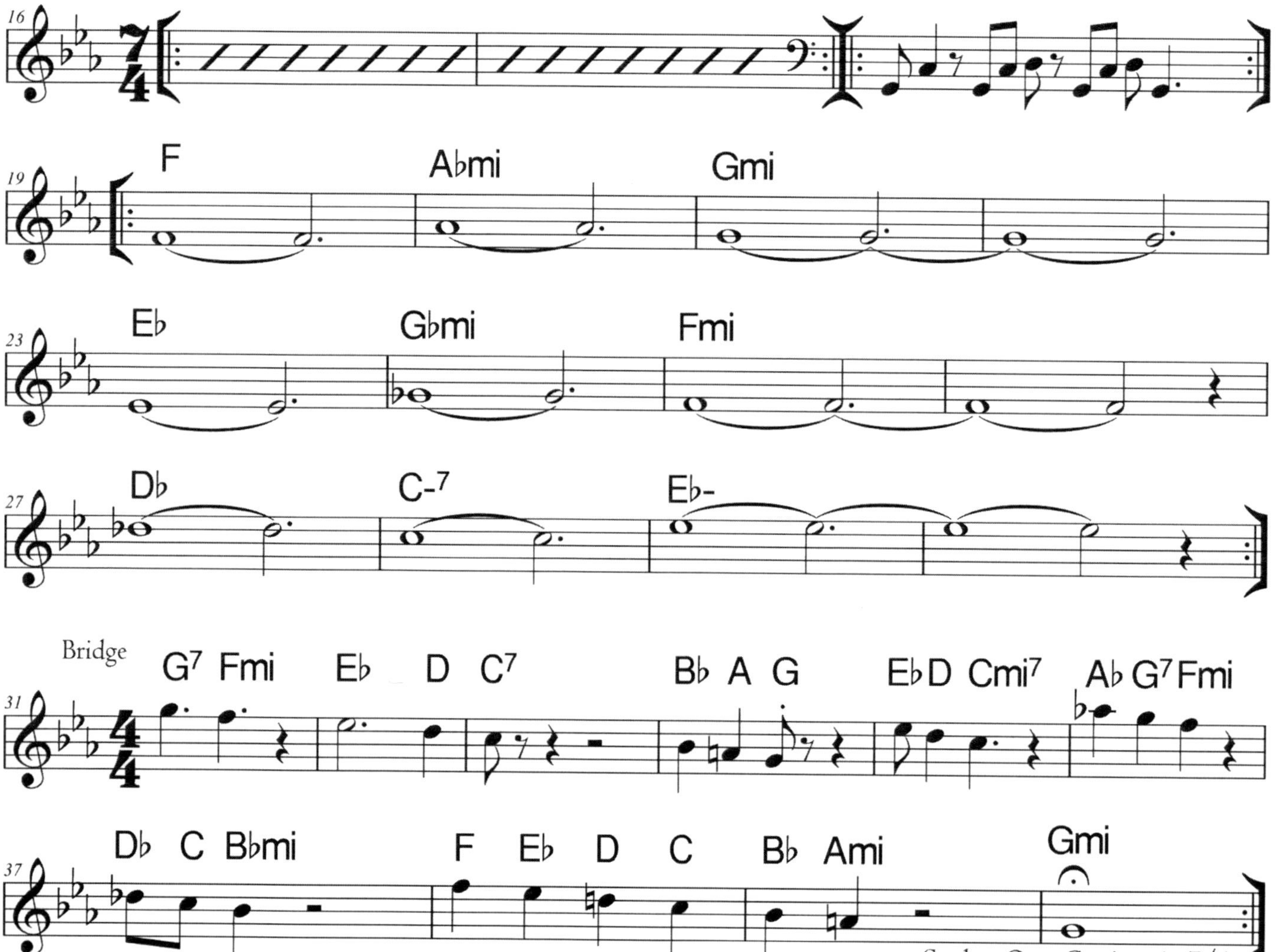

F
Abmi
Gmi
Eb
Gbmi
Fmi
Db
C-7
Eb-
Bridge
G7 Fmi
Eb
D C7
Bb A G
EbD Cmi7
Ab G7 Fmi
Db C Bbmi
F Eb D C
Bb Ami
Gmi

Soulos: Over G minor in 7/4.
Use bridge between soulos

Recorded on: Warren Oree & the Arpeggio Jazz Ensemble "Bambara"/SilkSkin Records, 2012
www.arpeggiojazzensemble.com

Perhaps This Wintertime

Recorded on: Larry McKenna "Profile"/Dreambox Media, 2009
www.melissagilstrap.com

Cmi7 F7 F7(♭9♯5) B♭ma7 Cmi7 Dmi7 Emi9 Fmi9 F♯mi9
29
come to me, win - ter trans - form.
E
Gmi9 C9 C7(♭9) Fma9 B♭13 Ami7 Dmi7 /C
33
I would hold you light - ly, like the yel- low au-tumn leaves that flame and burn so bright though
Bmi7(♭5) E7 Bmi7(♭5) D♯7 E7 Ami7 Cmi9 F13(♭9)
37
they will fade a - way and may - be you would too.
F
B♭ma7 E♭9(♯11) B♭mi7 Ami9 Ami7 A♭9 G13 G13(♯11)
41
May - be there will nev - er be the one love, just bright col - ors ev' - ry year...
Gmi7 Ami7 B♭ma7 C7(sus) C7(♭9) 1. F Emi9 Fmi9 F♯mi9
45
I will try to smile and hold the beau - ty dear.
2.
F D7(♯9) Gmi7 Ami7 B♭ma7 C7(sus) C7(♭9)
49
dear. I will try to smile and hold the beau - ty
Fma7 Fmi9 B♭9 E♭ma7 E9mi9 A♭9 D♭ma7 D♭mi9 G♭9 Fma7
53
dear.
rit.

The Perpetrator

Medium Swing

Michael Philip Mossman

♩= ca. 144

Recorded on: Art Blakey and the Jazz Messengers "Album of the Year"/Timeless SJP 155

C
Ab(13) G(13) Gb(13)
Fmi7(11) Bbmi7(11) C7(b5)
Fmi7(11) Bbmi7(11) C7(b5) F7 F7(#9)
mf
f
Ab13 A7(13) Bb7(13) E9(#11) Ebmi7 D7(#9 #5) G7(13 b9) C7(#9 Fmi7(11)
soloist
f
D
Fmi7(11) Bbmi11 C7(b5) Fmi11 Bbmi11 C7(b5) F7 Ab7 A7 Bb7
1.
Ebmi7 D7(#9 #5) G7(b9) Gb7(b9)
2.
Ebmi7 D7(#9 #5) F#mi7 F7(#9 #5)
E
Ema7 F7 Ema7 Eb7(#9 #5) Dma7 Eb7 Dma7
Dmi7 Bbmi7 Eb7 Dmi7 Abmi7 Db7 C7(#9) C#mi7 F#7 Fmi11 Ab7
F
Fmi11 Bbmi11 C7(b5) Fmi11 Bbmi11 C7(b5)
F7 Ab7 A7 Bb7 Ebmi7 D7(#9 #5) G7(b9) Gb9
Back to D for next soloist
after last solo D.S. al Coda
C7(#9) Fmi7(11)
add counterline
Vamp and Fade

Philadelphia Blues

Eric Mintel

Recorded on: Eric Mintel Quartet "Dynamo"
www.ericmintelquartet.com

Philadelphia Bound

Phrygian Love Theme

Medium Latin

Odean Pope

fine

sfz *sfz*

Solos

Ema Fma Ema Dmi

Melody is played 2x before Solos
and 2x after solos to fine.

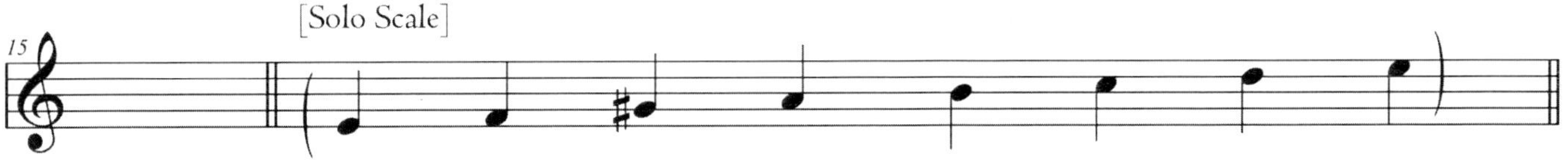

Recorded on: Odean Pope "The Ponderer"/Soul Note
www.odeanpope.com

Solos: F blues double time

Recorded on: Lynn Riley and the World-Mix "Say What"/Ru Ba Groov Records
www.lynnriley.com

Prayer for Mimi

Recorded on: The Paul Giess Group "U Suite U"/Paul Giess Music
www.paulgiessmusic.com

2.
E♭ma7(♯5) E7(♯9) Fma7(♯11) E♭7
33
Dmi7 C(sus4) B♭ma7(♯11) B♭ma7(♯11)/A
37
G(sus4) F°7 E♭ma7(♯11) F13
41
F♯(sus4) G(sus) A♭7 A7 B♭7
45
Ami7(♭6) A♭°
49
Cma7/G D7/F♯
53
Fma7(♯11) E7alt
57
E♭ma7(♯5) E7(♯9) Ami(♭6) E7(♯9)
61

Prince La Sha

Recorded on: Odean Pope "The Saxophone Shop"/Soul Note, 1986
www.odeanpope.com

Recorded on: Joey DeFrancesco "Project Freedom"/Mack Avenue
www.joeydefrancesco.com

Dmi7(♭5) G7(♯9) Cmi7
fine
Drums
8
G7(♭9) Cmi/G G7(♭9)
Cmi Fmi Cmi Cmi Fmi Cmi Cmi Fmi Cmi
Solos
Cmi Ab13
Dmi7(♭5) G7(♭9) Cmi7 Dmi7(♭5) G7(♯9)
Cmi7 Ab13
Dmi7(♭5) G7(♯9) Cmi7
Dmi7(♭5) G7(♯9) Cmi7 F13 Dmi7(♭5) G7(♯9)
Cmi Fmi Cmi Cmi Fmi Cmi Cmi Fmi Cmi

The Promise

Lee Smith

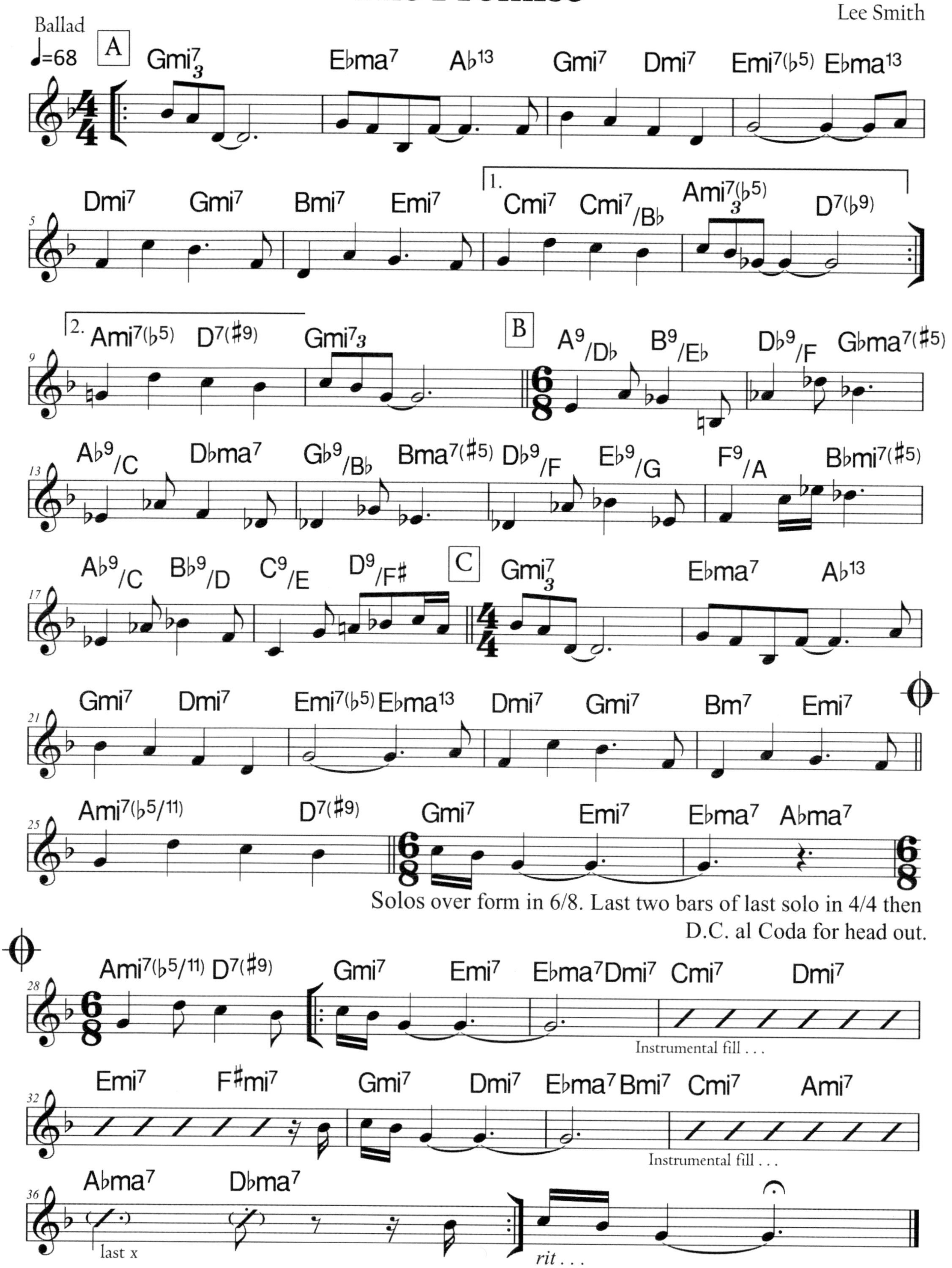

Ballad
♩=68
A
Gmi7 Ebma7 Ab13 Gmi7 Dmi7 Emi7(b5) Ebma13
Dmi7 Gmi7 Bmi7 Emi7
1. Cmi7 Cmi7/Bb Ami7(b5) D7(b9)
2. Ami7(b5) D7(#9) Gmi7
B
A9/Db B9/Eb Db9/F Gbma7(#5)
Ab9/C Dbma7 Gb9/Bb Bma7(#5) Db9/F Eb9/G F9/A Bbmi7(#5)
Ab9/C Bb9/D C9/E D9/F#
C
Gmi7 Ebma7 Ab13
Gmi7 Dmi7 Emi7(b5) Ebma13 Dmi7 Gmi7 Bm7 Emi7
Ami7(b5/11) D7(#9) Gmi7 Emi7 Ebma7 Abma7
Solos over form in 6/8. Last two bars of last solo in 4/4 then
D.C. al Coda for head out.
Ami7(b5/11) D7(#9) Gmi7 Emi7 Ebma7 Dmi7 Cmi7 Dmi7
Instrumental fill . . .
Emi7 F#mi7 Gmi7 Dmi7 Ebma7 Bmi7 Cmi7 Ami7
Instrumental fill . . .
Abma7 Dbma7
last x
rit . . .

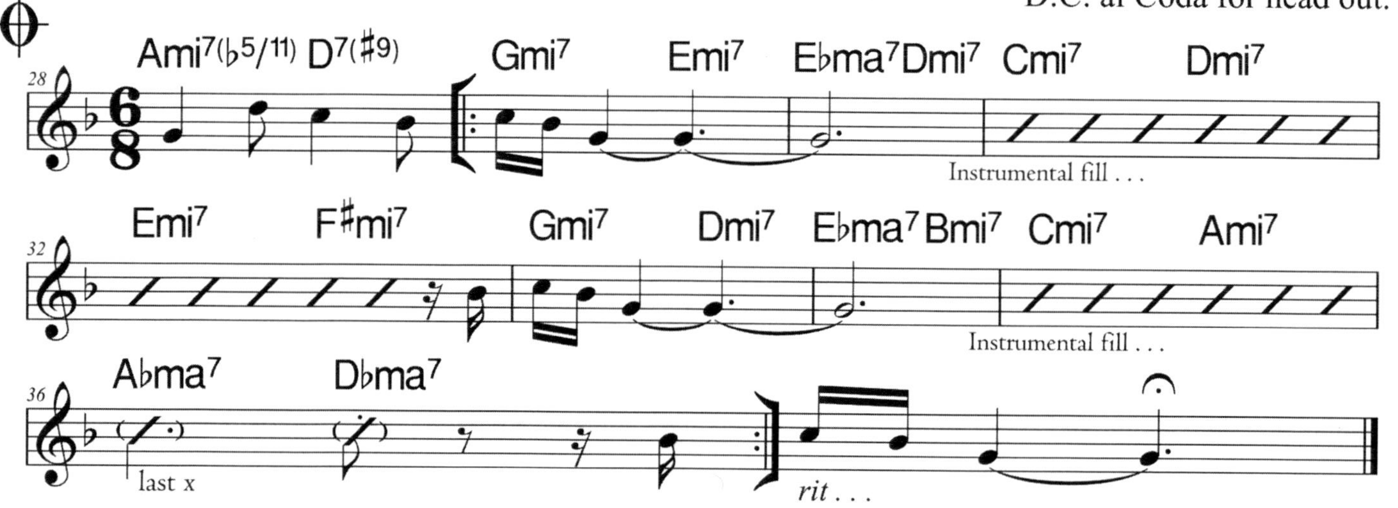

Recorded on: Lee Smith "Sittin' on a Secret"
www.leesmithmusic.com

Quid Pro Quo

Medium-Up Swing

Paul Gehman

Quietly into the Night

Michael Hoffman

Ballad

Recorded on: Michael Hoffman "Thinking out Loud"
www.drmikehoffman.com

Recorded on: Greg Snyder "In the State of Nature"
www.gregsnydermusic.com

Solos: AABA

Ray C

Leon Mitchell

Recorded on: Horace Parlan "On the Spur of the Moment"/Blue Note Records, 1961

Red Sky at Morning

Bop

Dave Renz

Recorded on: The Acoustic Groove Project "Plugged In"
www.daverenz.com

Ridge Ave Swing

Warren Oree

Recorded on: Warren Oree & the Arpeggio Jazz Ensemble "Touching Bass"
www.arpeggiojazzensemble.com

Behind the Mountain Wall

Warren Oree

Soulos: D minor. Cue spontaneous 16 bars of A minor at soloist discretion

Recorded on: Warren Oree & the Arpeggio Jazz Ensemble "Behind the Mountain Wall"/SilkSkin Records, 1992
www.arpeggiojazzensemble.com

Rio Crystal

Latin

Paul Colombo

Recorded on: Paul Colombo "Rio Crystal"
www.paulcolombomusic.com

C
Solos
Dmi
A+/D
Eb9(b5)
Dmi9
Dmi
A+/D
Emi7(b5)
A+7
Dmi
Cmi7
F7
Bbmaj7
Gmi7
Cmi7
B+7
Bb13
A+7
Dmi9
A+/D
Eb9(b5)
Dmi9
Bmi7(b5)
Bb7
A+7
Dmi
Bmi7(b5)
Bb7
A+7(#9)
Dmi
D
Gmi
D+/G
Gmi7
C9
Bbmi7
C#mi7
F#7
Bma7
Bb+7
Ebmi9
Ab13
Ami
E7(b9)
Bmi7
Cmi7(b5)
C#mi11
C7(b5)
Dmi11
Db7(b5)
Cmi7
B+7
Bb13
A7alt
D.C. al fine

Rooms Etude Part III

Eddie L. Hill

Straight Eighths

B
G7(♭9)/C
F7(♯9)
C7(sus4)/G
E♭mi(ma7)
B♭6/9/D
E♭7(♯9)
(horns)

fine

Solos

After Solos D.S. al Fine

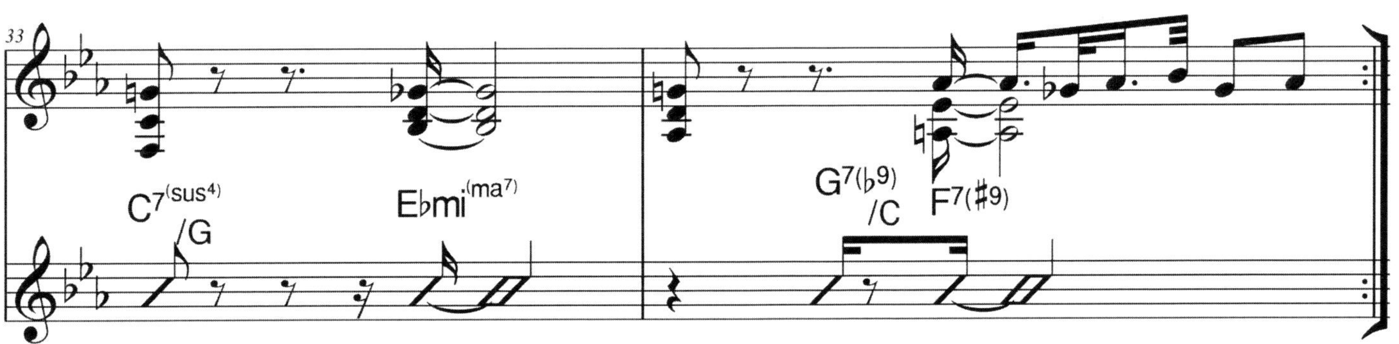

The Ruling Passion

Fran Lawton

Ballad

♩=63

A
B7(♭5) E7(♭5) Emi7(♭5) E♭7 A♭7(♭5)

4 B7(♭5) E7(♭5) Emi7(♭5) E♭7 A♭7(♭5) A7 D7

8 G7(♭5) C9 Fma7 B♭7(#9/♭9) B7 B♭ma7

B
12 Gmi7 Cma7 E♭mi7 D7(♭5) A♭+7 B♭ma7

A
15 B7(♭5) E7(♭5) Emi7(♭5) E♭7 A♭7(♭5) B7(♭5) E7(♭5)

19 Emi7(♭5) E♭7 A♭7(♭5) A7 D7 G7(♭5) C9

23 Fma7 B♭7(#9/♭9) B7 B♭ma7

Sam Meets James

Robert Colligan

Recorded on: Big Swing Face "Mutant Mosquitoes from New Jersey"

www.colliganbobmusic.com

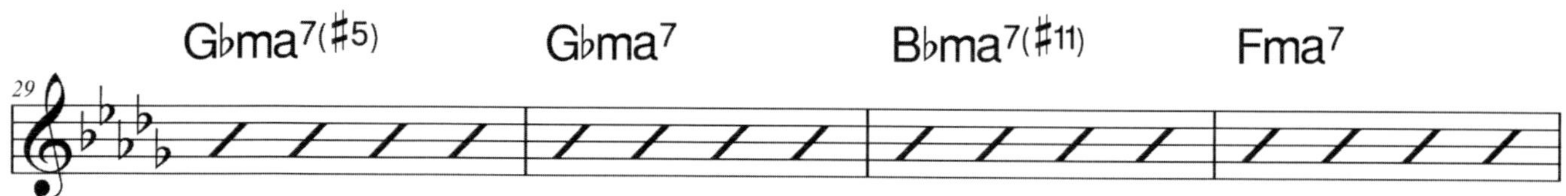

After Solo D.C. al Coda

Recorded on: Art Blakey and the Jazz Messengers "Album of the Year"/Timeless SJP 155

D
Ebmi7 D7(#9 #5) Dbmi7 C7(#9 #5) C7(13 b9) B6/9 Bb7(13 b9)
Bb7(13 b9) Db7(#9 #5) F7(#9 #5) Bb7(#9 #5) Ebmi11 F#7(13) F7(#9) Ema7(#11) Ebma7(#11)
to solos
Ebma7(#11) Ema7(#11) D6/9 Eb6/9
last time
Ebma7 Ema7(#11) E6/9 Eb6(9)(#11)
fine
E
Solos
Bbmi7 Eb7(#9 #5) Abmi7 Bb7(#9 #5) Ebmi7 Dbmi7
Bmi7 Adim(ma7)/G# C#mi11 C7(#11)
Bmi7 Bb7(#9 #5) Ama7 Fmi7 Bb7(13 b9) Ebma7 D7(#9 #5)
F
C#mi7 D#mi7 Ema7 Bb7(#9 #5) Bma7(#11) E7 Fmi7(b5) Bb7(#9 #5) Ebma7 Ema7 Ebma7
G
C#7(sus) Eb7(sus) E7(sus) Ami9 Ema7(#11) F#ma7(#11)
Ama7(#11) C7(#11 #9) Ebmi7 D7(#9 #5) Dbmi7 C7(#9 #5) Bma7 E7
solos continue
last time only
Ebmi11 F#7(13) F7(#9 #5) Ema7 Ebma7 Ema7 Ebma7 Ebma7
D.S.al fine
mf

Sasha's Song

Kat Souponetsky

Medium Ballad

♩ = 100

Gmi7(add9) | Gmi7(♭6) | E♭/G | Ami7(♭5)

F7(add13) | E♭ma7 | Cmi7 | A♭/C

Fmi7(add9) | Fmi7(♭6) | D♭/F | Gmi7(♭5)

E♭7(add13) | D♭ma7 | B♭mi7 Gmi7(♭5)

1. Gmi7

2. Fmi7 *fine* Gmi7

(vamp)

After solos, D.C. al fine

Sassy Shuffle

Shuffle

Karen Rege

Say No More

Julian Horner

Recorded on: The Julian Hartwell Project "The Julian Hartwell Project"/Julian Hartwell Music/ASCAP
www.julianhartwellmusic.com

Break
B
Fmi11
Gbma7(#11)
Fmi11
Fmi11
Dbma13
/C
Bbmi7
Ab9
Cmi7(b5)
Cmi7(b5)
Gbma9(#11)
Ebmi9
Fmi9
Ebmi9
Fmi9
Break
Ab9
Dbma13
Gmi7
Bma13
Cmi7(b5)
Cmi7(b5)
Db6/9
Fmi13
D.S. to Solos on form.
After last time, use Intro as Outro vamp

Saying Goodbye

Music by John David Simon
Lyrics by Per Salemyr

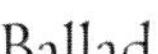

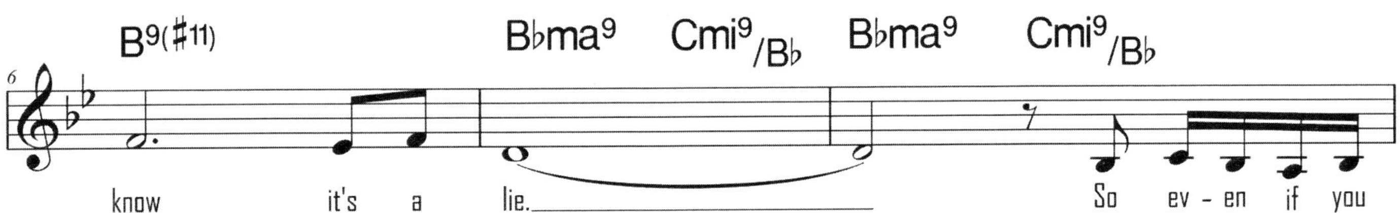

Recorded on: "John David Simon and Friends with Clark Terry & Etta Jones"/WarmGroove Records, 2009
www.johndavidsimon.com

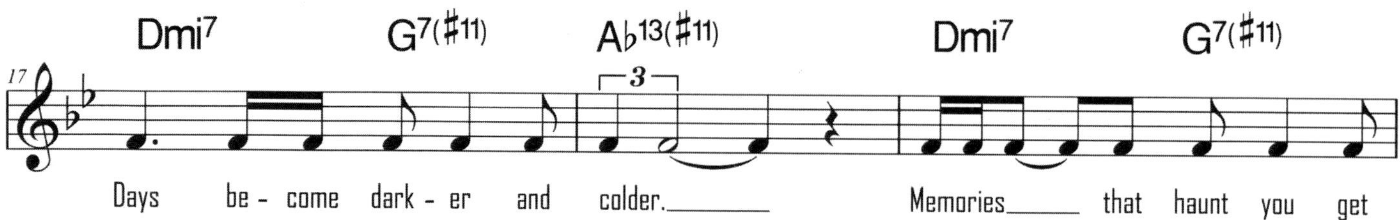
Dmi7 G7(♯11) A♭13(♯11) Dmi7 G7(♯11)
17
3
Days be - come dark - er and colder.
Memories that haunt you get

A♭13(♯11) Emi7 A7(♯11) Dmi11 G+7
20
3
3
bolder.
Nights with out sleep make you older.
Is

Emi7 A7(♯11) B♭13(♯11) A♭ma9
23
this what you want from your life? There's ne - ver an - y good in a sad goodbye

D♭ma9(♯11) A♭ma9 D♭ma9(♯11)
26
and yet when your eyes at last are dry you're

G♭ma9(♯11) B9(♯11) B♭ma9
29
through! Then it's time that you say good - bye!

Scare the Ghost

Michelle Lordi &
Tim Motzer

Recorded on: "Eidolon"/1K Recordings
www.michellelordi.com | www.1krecordings.com/artists/tim-motzer

G Ami
why did n't you___ come see___ me?
Chorus: G C Fma7 G
Scare_____ the ghosts_ out of my head
Scare_____ the ghosts_ and
G C6 F G
go_____ to bed
Ami G C
In the dream he said to me, If you know this place,_ why
Fma9 G C
didn't_ you come see__ me? If you know this place why didn't_ you__come see__ me?
Fma7 G Ami
Scare_____ the ghosts Scare__ the
Ami G C Fma7
3
ghosts___ out of my
G C
hold F
Scare_____ the ghosts out of my head
Solo:
G Ami G C

F G G C F
G Ami G C
F G G C F
solo ends
G Ami G C
Chorus:
Scare the ghosts out of my head
Fma7 G C
Will I meet you in the
Fma7 G Ami
sec-cond sleep? Will I meet you in the
Ami G C Fma7
sec-ond sleep? Scare the ghosts out of my head.
G G C F
Scare the ghosts and go to bed
G Ami C Fma7
Will I meet you in the sec-ond sleep?
G Ami Ami Ami7
cue next
I'll sec-ond sleep?

Seek First

Intro - [piano (octaves) and bass]
AJ Luca
Up-Tempo Swing
B♭13(♭9♭5)
E♭ma9(♯11)
Fmi (ma7♭5)
B♭7(♯9♯5)
E♭13(♯11)
A7(♯9♯5)
Dmi7
G7alt
G7alt
B♭13(♭9♭5)
E♭ma9(♯11)
Solos
C7alt
B♭7alt
E♭ma9(♯11)
Fmi7(♭5)
B♭7alt
E♭13(♯11)
A7alt
Dmi7
G7alt
C7alt
B♭7alt
E♭ma9(♯11)

The Self I Used to Be, but Never Knew I Was, and Now I Am Again

Fran Lawton

Recorded on: Mtown Jazz "Live at the Pinelands Jazz Festival 2015"
www.mtown.bandcamp.com

Serendib Lasio

Jim Miller

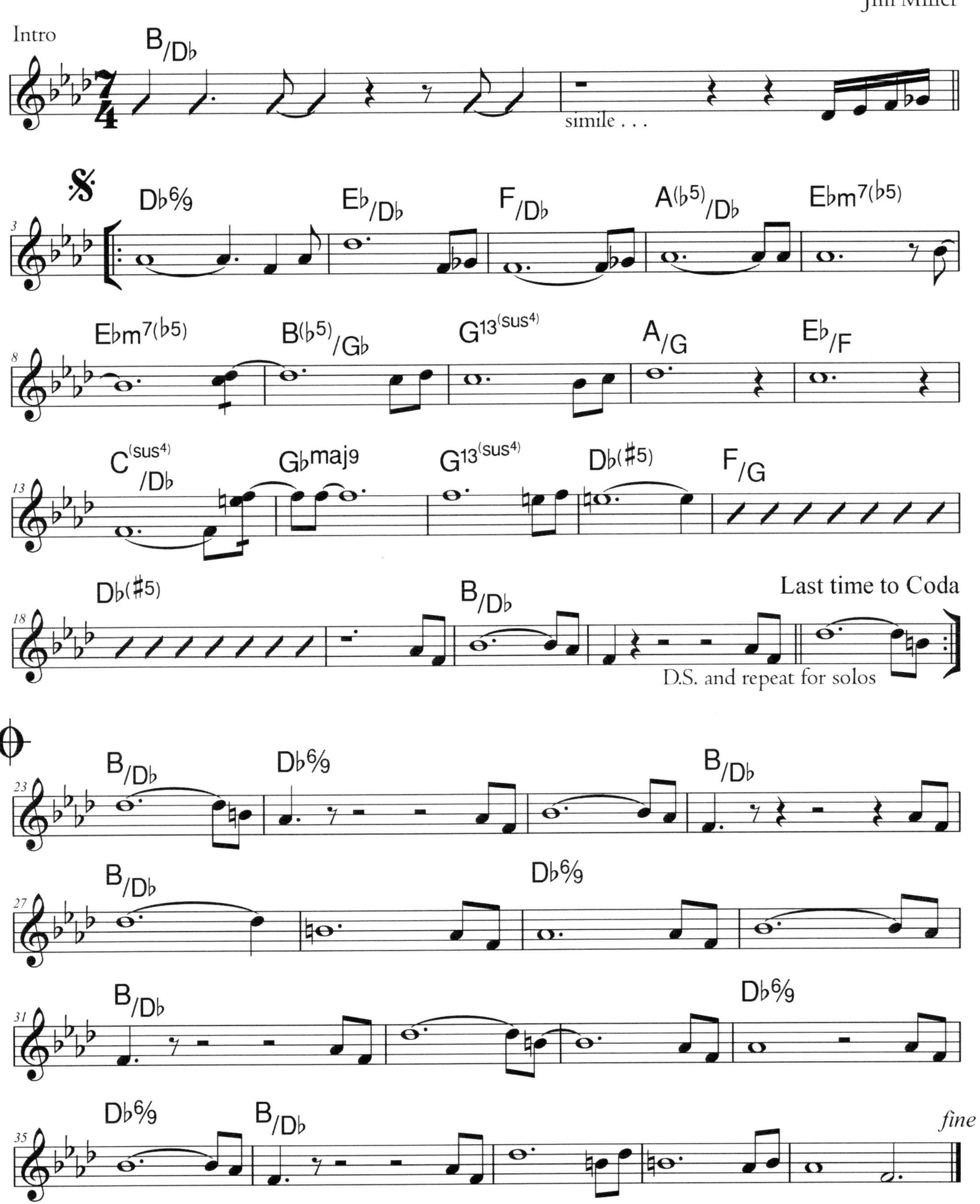

Recorded on: "... It's Another"/Dreambox Media
www.dreamboxmedia.com

The Shade of the Cedar Tree

Christian McBride

As played on Christian McBride's "Gettin' to It"/Verve Records 314 523 989-2
www.christianmcbride.com

Shades of Green

Recorded on: Eddie Green "Shades of Green"/Dreambox Media
www.dreamboxmedia.com

Fmi7
Bbmi7
Ab6
Gbma7
Ema7(#11)
Fmi7
Bbmi7
Abmi7
Gmi7
Gmi7
C9
Fmi7
D7(#9)
Bbmi7
Abmi11
Gb13
C+7
Fmi7
D
Bbmi11
Gmi11
Ami11
Gbmi11
Gmi11
Emi11
Ebmi11
Ebmi9
C7
Solos
Fmi7
Bbmi7
Fmi7
Bbmi7
Bbmi7
Fmi7
Db13
C7(#9)
Fmi7
D7(#9)
Bbmi7
Gbma7/Ab
Abma7/Gb
C7(#9)
Fmi7
C7(#9)

Shopping Barra Blues

Lynn Riley

Recorded on: Lynn Riley and the World-Mix "Say What"/Ru Ba Groov Records
www.lynnriley.com

Gma7
Bmi7(♭5)
E7
Ami7
B♭o
Bmi7
Bmi7(♭5)
E7
Ami7
C6
D13
C13(♯11)
B♭7
8va
E7
A7(♭9)
Solos over A, Cue B then D.C. al Coda
A7(sus4)
A♭7(sus4)
D7(sus4)
D7(sus4)
D7(sus4)
D7(sus4)
8va
Gmi7
fine

Shorter Street

Edward "Eddie" Green

Recorded on: Catalyst "Unity"/Muse Records

Sierra Nicole's Bossa

Medium Bossa

Keith Javors

♩=98

Fma7 C♯mi7 Cma7(♭5)

Ami7 Dmi7 Cmi7 Fmi7

B♭mi7 E♭mi7 A♭mi7 G7(♭9) Cmi7

1. C♯(sus13) B(sus13) A(sus13) G(sus13) Emi7

2. C♯(sus13) B(sus13) A(sus13) G(sus13) Emi7

Dmi7 E♭ma7(♭5) Dmi7 E♭ma7(♭5)

double time feel

Dmi7 E♭ma7 Dmi7 E♭ma7 C/E(add9)

B∅(9) B♭9 Ami9 A♭ma7(♭5) C♯mi7 Cma7(♭5)

Recorded on: Keith Javors "Mo' City Jungle"/Zoho and Oleg Kireyev & Keith Javors "Rhyme and Reason"/Inarhyme Records
www.keithjavors.com

Silver Earrings
♩=85
Valdea D. Jennings
for BMJ
Intro/verse
E♭9 Dmi7 Gmi9 C7
C7 F6
♩=70 Fma7 Gmi7 Ami7 Gmi7 Gmi7(♭5) C7 Ami7 D7(♯9)
Gm7(♭5) Dmi9 Gmi7 Gmi7(♭5) G♭13
1. Fma9 G♭9(♯11)
2.
Bridge
Gmi11
Dmi13 G7 G♭9(♯11) C7 Fma9 F9 B♭ma9 Ami7
E♭9 Dmi7 Gmi9 G♭9 Dmi11 G♭13
Fma7 Gmi7 Ami7 B♭ma7 Gmi9(♭5) C7 Fma9 F♯o7
Gmi9(♭5) Dmi9 Gmi7 G♭9 C7 F

S'Life

Intro: Rubato

Jason Fifield

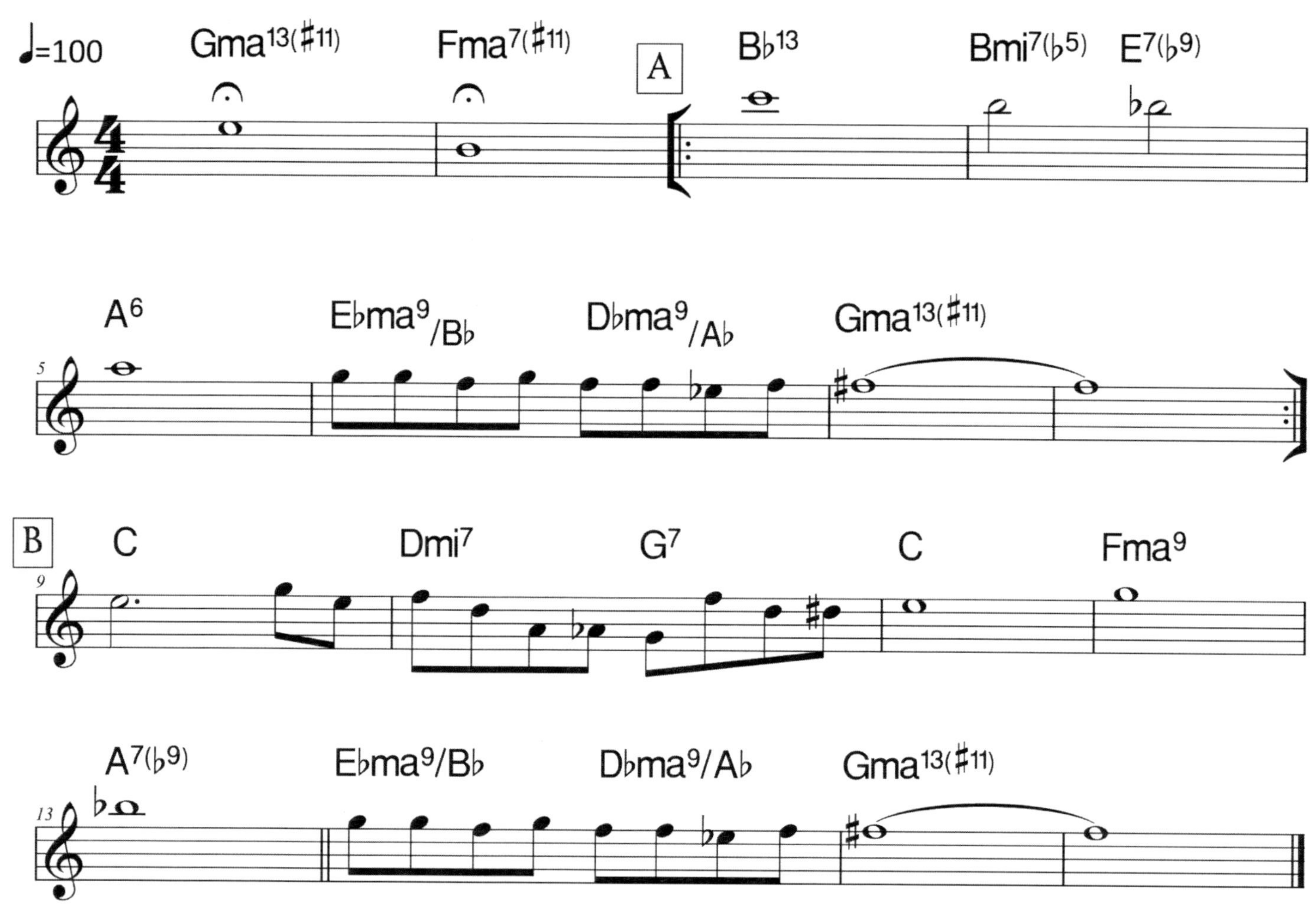

Tag last 4 bars for coda

Recorded on: Orrin Evans "Knowing Is Half the Battle"
www.slifeproductions.com

Recorded on: Vince Tampio "Sound Plan"
www.vincetampio.com

Solo vamp 1 - Rock feel
Ad. lib. Groove
E
A7(♯9)
F
Ami6
G7 Ami6
B♭7 Ami7
G7 Ami7
Solo vamp 2 - (background parts on cue)
G
A7(13)
C7
E♭7 G7
B♭7 C7 B♭7
B♭7 C7 B♭7
C7
B♭7
Break
N.C.
D7(13) C7(13)
B7(9)

Smelly

Slow Ballad

Uri Caine

Recorded on: Uri Caine "Siren"/Winter & Winter

www.uricaine.com

Smooth Sailing

Dave Wilson

Recorded on: Dave Wilson "There Was Never"/ZOHO Music 2016
www.davewilsonmusic.org

Snaggletooth

Fast Swing

Uri Caine

Recorded on: Uri Caine "Live at the Village Vanguard"/Winter & Winter

www.uricaine.com

Medium Swing

So Smile

Raimundo Santos

So Tired

Latin

Bobby Timmons

Solos: A thru C
Then D.S. for head out.
Ending: D.C. fade on intro

Solomon's Serenade

William R. Davis, Jr.

Recorded on: William R. Davis, Jr. "William R. Davis, Jr.,'s First CD"/Flute of the Spirit Publishing/ASCAP

Soul-Etude

Elliott Levin

Long live the Wild Tcholatoulis!!!
Long live the Black Indians-
run Sun Ra Mummer numbers
rump-us romantically
waxing poetic and forever . . .
Prophetic and
so clever how they grow live dolls in Bali . . .
Knees and lips and eyes are saying and
gracing their sway in their sacred play . . .
while everyone's just doing the best they can . . .
Light Bright Buddha-B-Day idea . . . Sri Lankan light fest. . .
Feast for other eyes for size of
any benevolent God.

rim shots . . .
rum shots . . .
Cake-walk down the line e-quipped and
tripping on shots . . . from the hip . . .
and the hipper they are . . .
the happier they feel the fall
from the grace-less place
of separation of state (of being) . . .
from religion

Ingenuity is the- (root)
mother of-all-necessary-evils we love
to hate . . .
We contemplate, relate
and sing, but rarely keep our needy wants
-in-waiting in Lady-Lord's
audacious space
each one
defines
their soul.

-excerpts of 'Soul-Etude' from 'Does It Swing'
Elliott Levin 1996

Recorded on: Tyrone Hill & Elliott Levin Quartet "Soul-Etude"/CIMP Ltd #206
www.elliottlevin.com

Speedball

Lee Morgan

By Lee Morgan

Spiral

Dave Wilson

Recorded on: Dave Wilson "Spiral"/Summit Records, 2010
www.davewilsonmusic.org

C
A7(♭9)
G7(♭9)
[2x]
D Solos
Cma6(9)
D/C
Cma6(9)
1.2.3.
4.
D♭9
E7
E9
F♯9
B7alt
Fmi9
F(sus9)
Ami7(♭5) D7 Fmi7 B♭/E
E
A7(♭9)
G7(♭9)
After Solos D.S. al Coda

Ami7(♭5)
D7
A♭mi7(♭5)
D♭7(♯9)
Cma6(9)
D/C
Cma6(9)
Cma6(9)
D♭9
1. E7
2. E9
F7(♯9)
B♭7(♭9)
Cue next
(sax trades 8's with piano)
B♭7(♭9)
2x
cresc . . .
fine

St. Somebody

Jef Lee Johnson

Recorded on: Jef Lee Johnson "St. Somebody"/Dreambox Media
www.dreamboxmedia.com

Sunday Afternoon

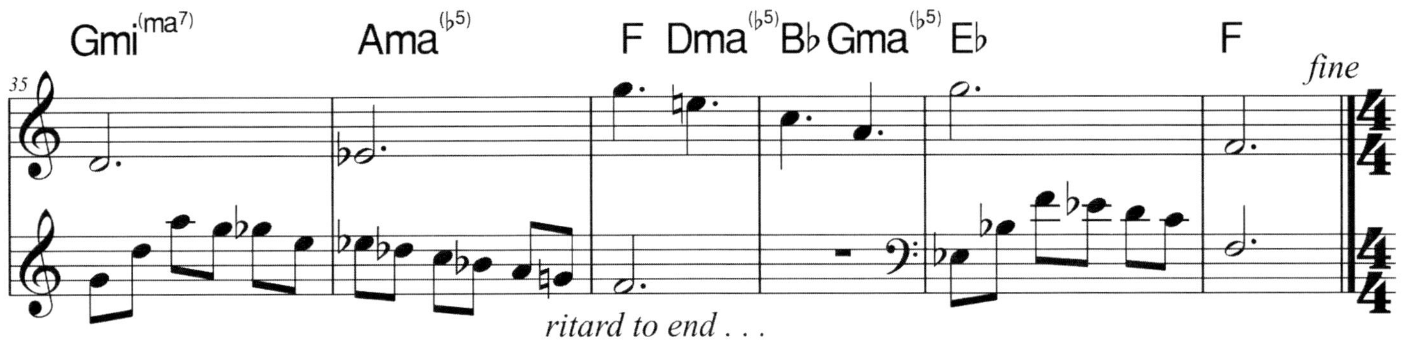

♩=200 (In any solo chorus: Notated figures, in whole or in fragments, are at the discretion of the soloist or accompanist)

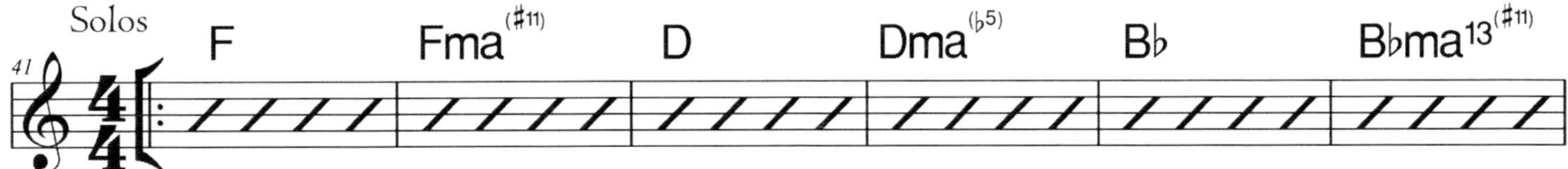

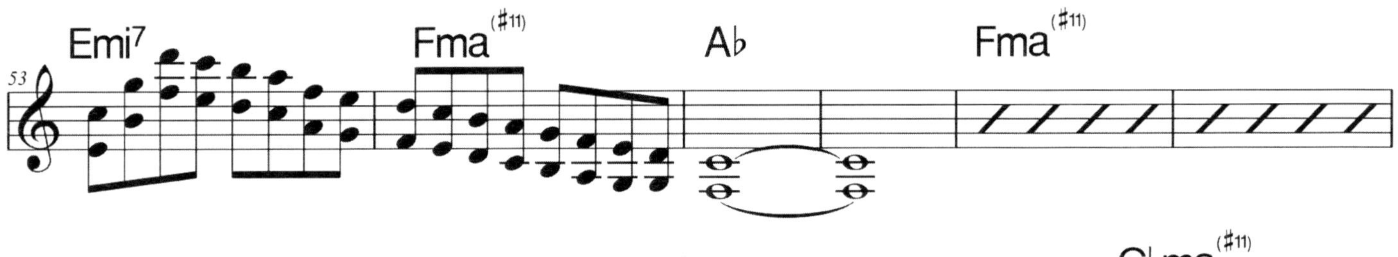

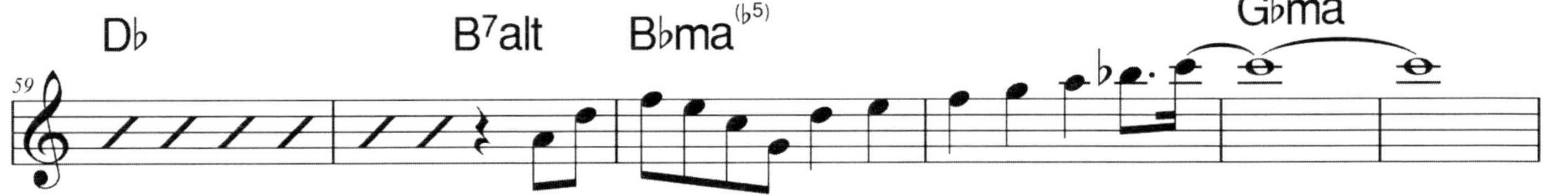

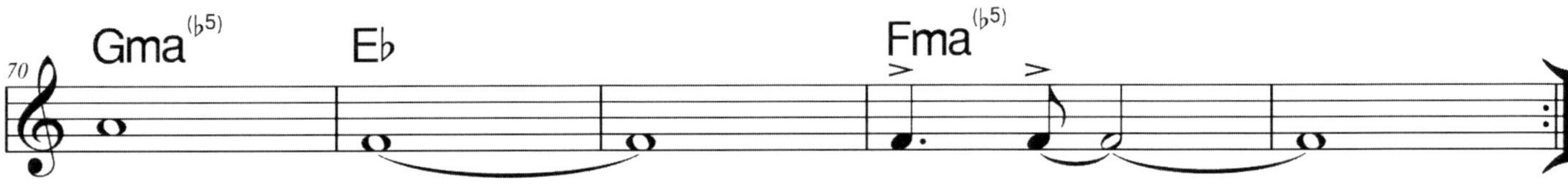

Last solo: [noodle and retard to return to rubato head]

Sunday Blues

Adam Faulk

Sunday Sermon on Mars, Homage to Sun Ra

Bert Harris

Swing

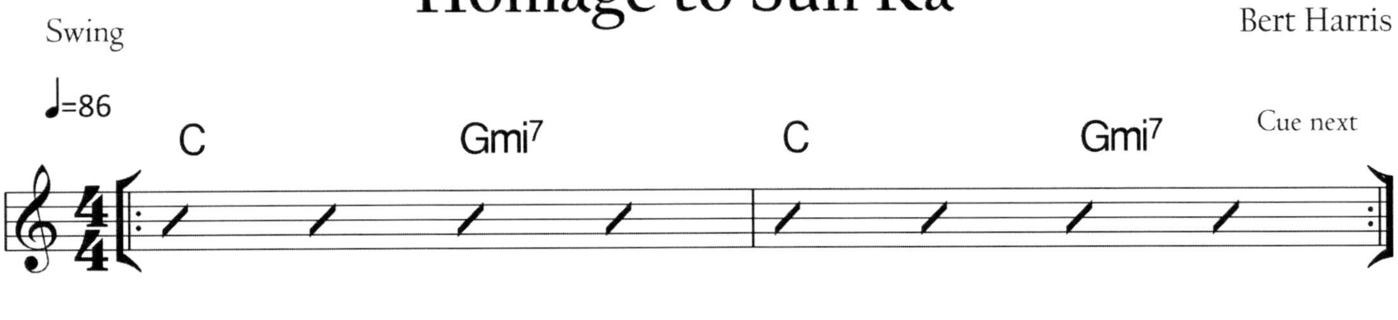

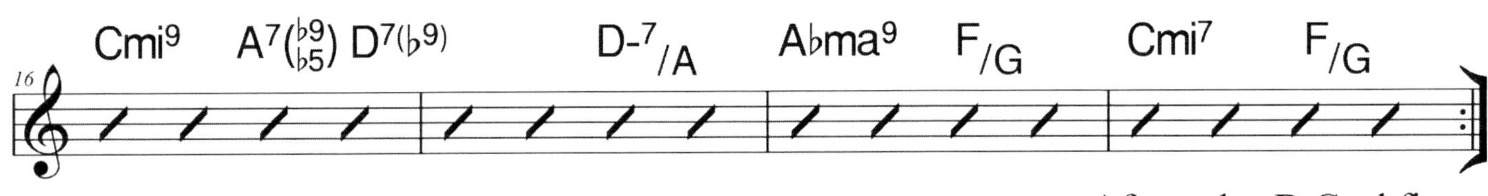

After solos D.C. al fine

Suzy's Upright

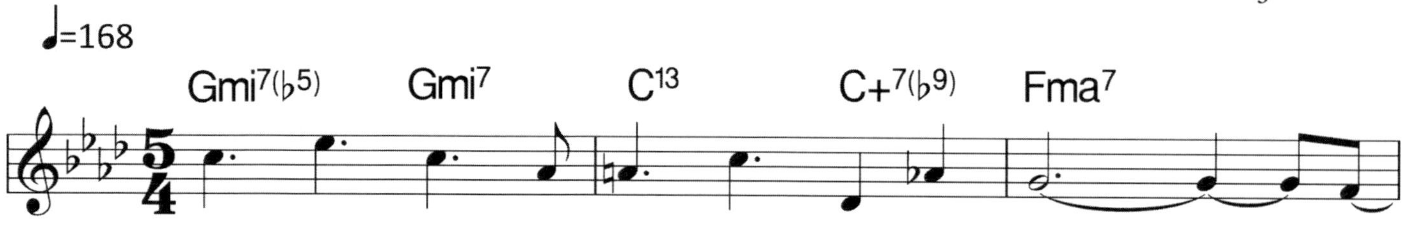

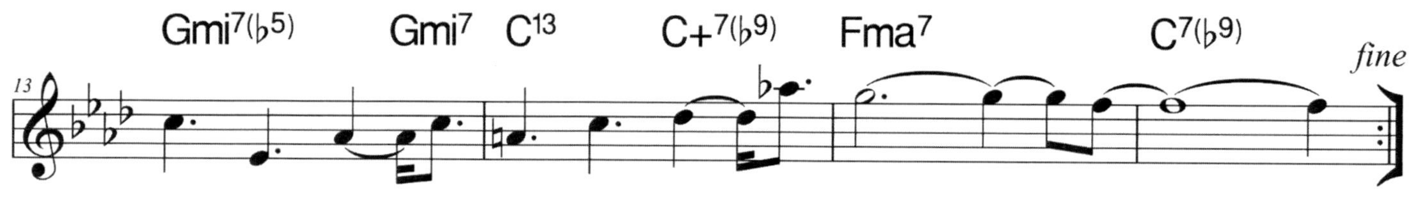

Recorded on: Miller Time "If It's Not One Thing . . ."/Dreambox Media
www.dreamboxmedia.com

TACTICAL STRATEGIES no.1

by Julius Masri, 2016

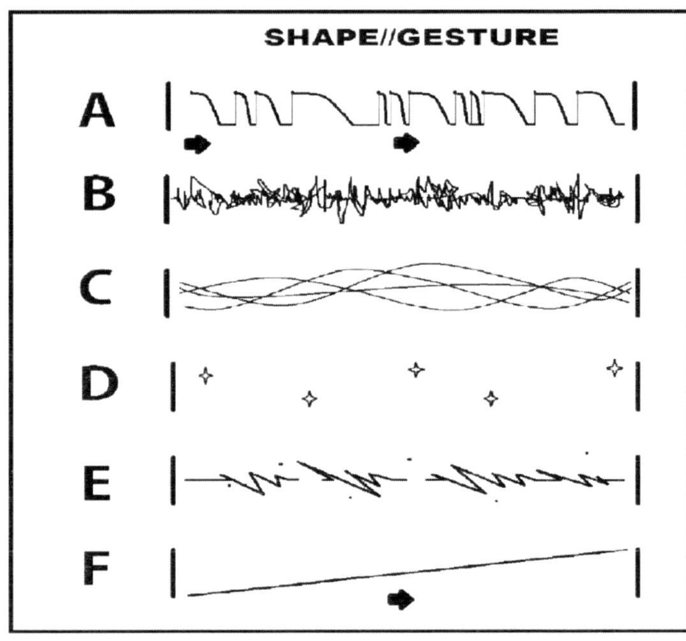

This piece is intended for, but not restricted to, six instrumentalists. A conductor may be required, although a timekeeper may be designated from amongst the performers. Each musician is initially assigned a specific Shape/Gesture designation: A through F. At the end of each movement, the performer will switch to the next designation: A to B, B to C, F cycling back to A.

There are a total of eight movements, (1 through 8), each lasting a fixed length of time, to be performed by all musicians in sequence. Each movement represents a certain density of sound that the musicians must interpret through their currently assigned Shape/Gesture designations.

Movement 8, (Spoken Dialogue), may be performed from an agreed upon source material, but the execution must adhere to the assigned Shape/Gesture designation. As is in the previous movements, musicians must pay attention to the densities and sonorities that occur in this section.

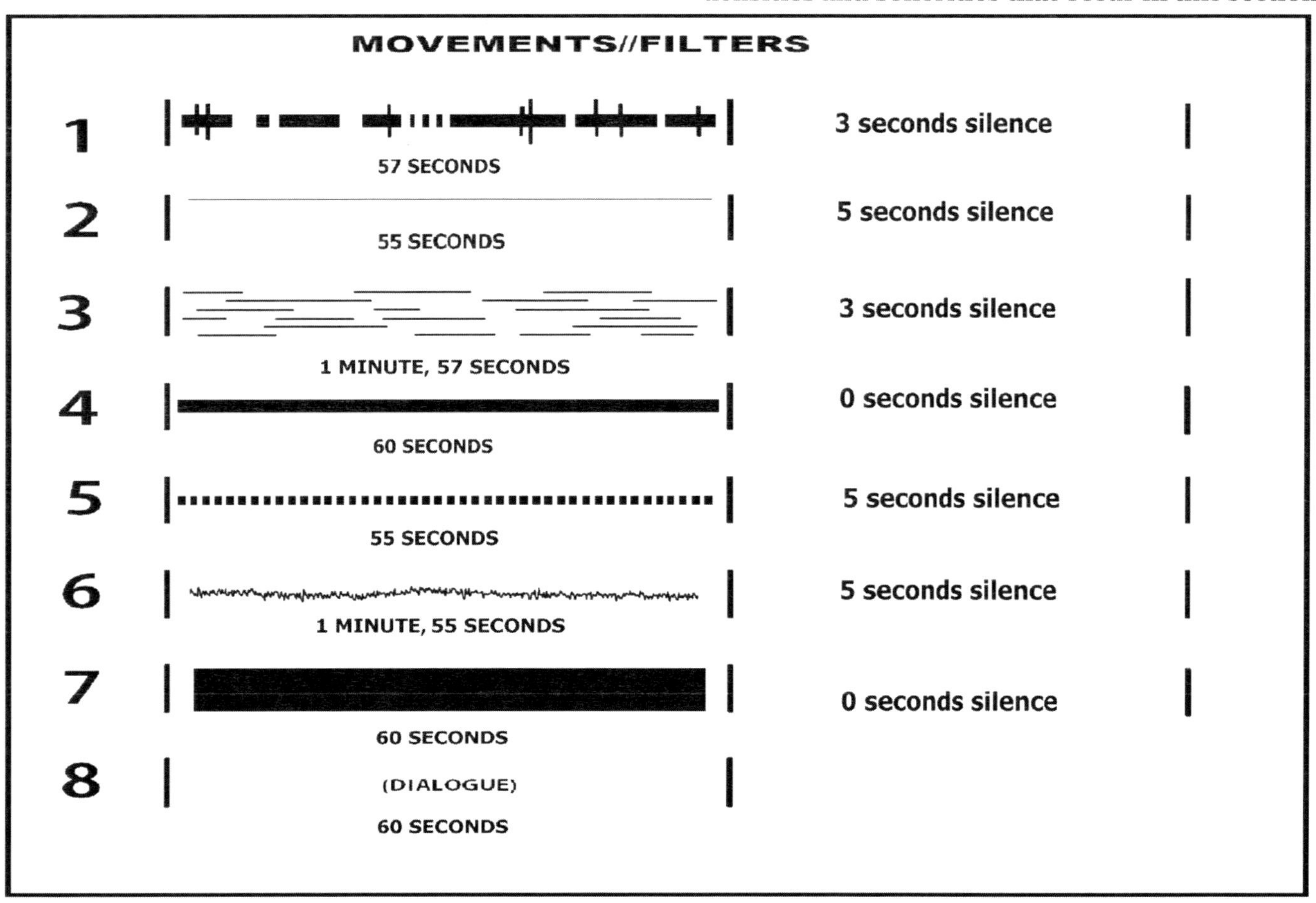

Tangibility

♩ = 210

Benjamin Sutin

Recorded on: Klazz-Ma-Tazz "Tangibility"/One Trick Dog Records
www.bensutinmusic.com

E7(#11) Fmi E7(#11) E°7
Fmi C#°7 Dmi D♭ma7 B°7 Cmi
ff
Fmi C7(♭9) D♭
mp mf mp
Fmi G7(♭9) A+ A+
fine
mf cresc . . f ff fff
(can be in either 6/4 or 5/4)
Solos
Dmi A7(♭9) A♭ma7 C#°7 Dmi E♭°7 Emi7 Fmi/E
Fmi7 A♭°7 Ami7 Fma7(#5) D♭ma7 G♭ma7 Emi9 Dmi9 G♭ma7 E♭mi7(♭5)
D♭7(#9) E°7 Fmi E7(#11) Fmi E7(#11) Fmi
E7(#11) Fmi E7(#11) E°7 Fmi C#°7 Dmi D♭ma7 B°7
Cmi Fmi C7(♭9) D♭
Fmi G7(♭9) A+
After solos D.S. al Fine

Tap Shoe Blues

Half Time Feel

Pamela Hetherington &
Jason Long

Tarshish

Uri Caine

Recorded on: Uri Caine "Siren"/Winter & Winter
www.uricaine.com

Teardrops for Jimmy

Music by Dave Burrell
Lyrics by Monika Larsson

Recorded on: Dave Burrell "Black Spring"/Marge Recordings, 1977
www.daveburrell.com

Bmi7 E7 Bb mi7 Eb7 Ami7 D7
26
Sha - dows fell on your dus - ky skin, see - ing you was quite

Gb7 Bma7
32
3
rare Your face, I swear, I saw right

Bmi(ma7) Bbmi7 A°
35
there in my dream you sang a - long

Abmi7 Db7 Bbmi7(b5) Eb7
38
jazz up - town we al - ways came a - round I

Abmi7 Abmi7 A7 Bbmi7 Bmi7 E7 Bbmi7 Eb7(b9) Abmi7
42
3
swear, you sat right there a - lone, se - rene, deep

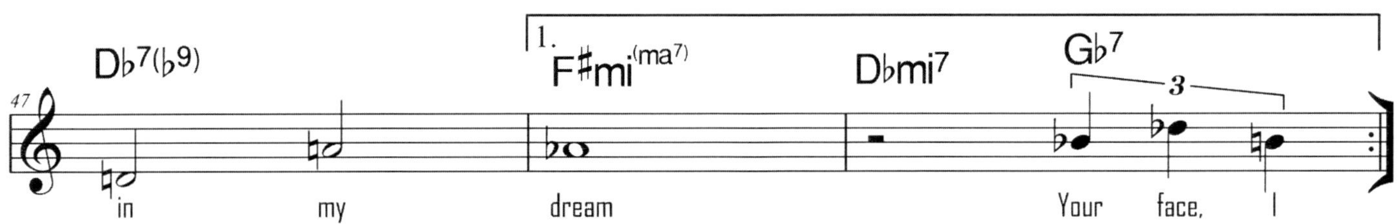
1.
Db7(b9) F#mi(ma7) Dbmi7 Gb7
47
3
in my dream Your face, I

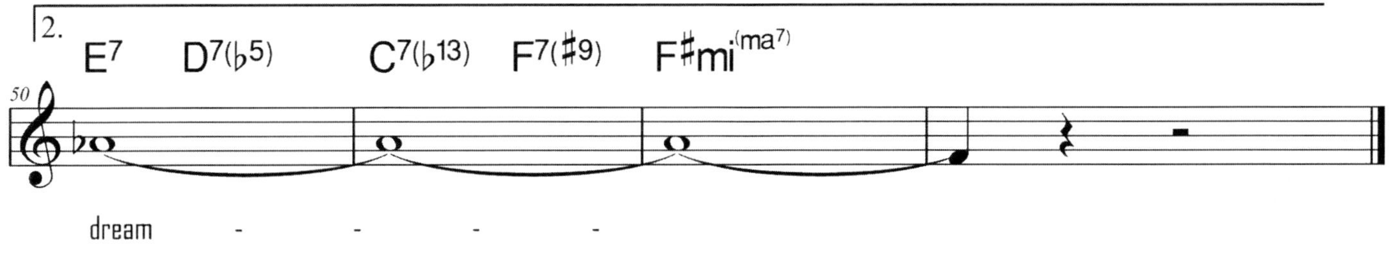
2.
E7 D7(b5) C7(b13) F7(#9) F#mi(ma7)
50
dream - - - -

Teddy Makes 3

Bill "Mr. C" Carney

Recorded on: Trudy Pitts "These Blues of Mine"/Prestige

That's How I Feel about You

These Are the Good Ol' Days

New Orleans-ish

Jason Fraticelli

www.jasonfraticelli.com

D♭7 C7 D♭7
I These days are better than before tell me could you ever ask for
D♭7 D7 D♭7
more Happiness as far as I can see better days are here for you and
D♭7 C7 D♭7
me Everything as right as right can be
D♭7 D♭7 B7 A7 G7
golden days are here for you and me We're
C
B♭7
gonna have a big ol' party yeah We're gonna have a good time We're
B♭7
gonna have a big ol' party yeah cause these are the good ol' days We're
1. 2.
days HEY!

This Moment's Sweetness

Music & lyrics by Rhenda Fearrington
Inspired by Marilyn Sanford

Recorded on: Rhenda Fearrington "This Moment's Sweetness"
www.heartofourhome.com

2.
Ama7
D/A
Db/F
F#mi7
G7(sus)
Hold on I want this mo- ment to
Cma7
Emi7 Db/F
F#mi7
G7(sus)
last
go slow don't speak don't move so
3
Bmi7
E7
Eb7
Dma7
Bmi7
fast
by the day's light you'll be
F#mi7
E/G#
Dma7
E7
free to go wher- ev - er you choose but now I need you here til the next time
Ama7
Solo
Dma7
Bmi7
F#mi7
D.S. al Coda
E/G#
Dma7
E7
Ama7
D/A
Ama7
Db/F
Ama7 E/G#
F#mi7
E
Dma7
Bmi7
By the day light you'll be
F#mi7
E/G#
Dma7
E7
free to go where ev - er you choose but now I need you here til the next time
rit . . .
Ama7
D/A
E7(sus)
Ama7

This Way Out

Johnnie Valentino

Recorded on: Michael Pedicin "Everything Starts Now"/Jazz Hut Records
www.johnnievalentino.com

Three Miles Out

Robert "Bootsie" Barnes

Recorded on: Don Patterson "Why Not"/Muse Records 1538 and Boostie Barnes "Boppin' Around the Center"/Harvest

www.bootsiebarnes.com

Time to Kill

Johnathan Blake

Recorded on: Johnathan Blake "The Eleventh Hour"/Blasak Music
www.johnathanblake.com

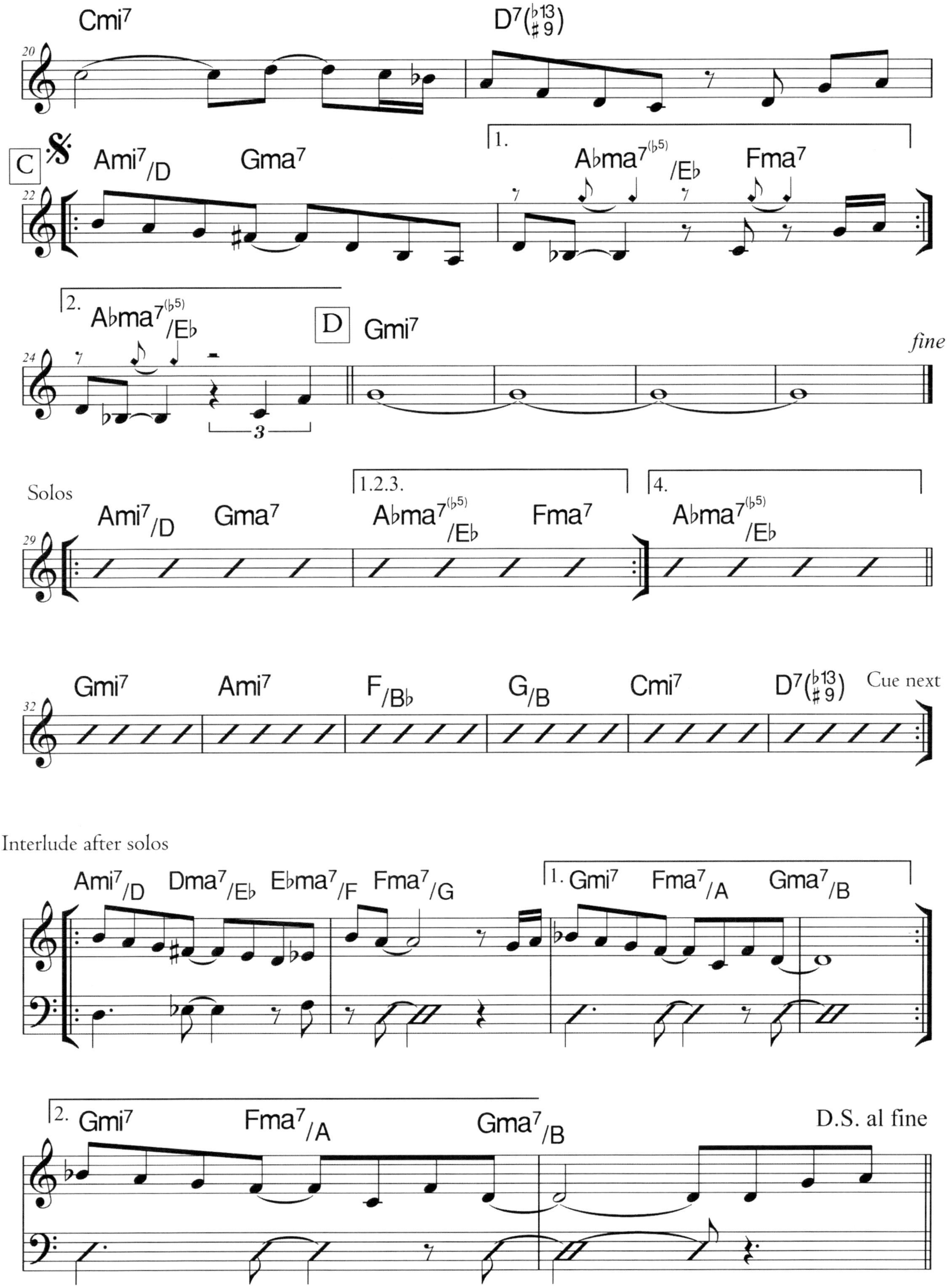

Cmi7
D7(♭13 ♯9)
C
Ami7/D
Gma7
1.
A♭ma7(♭5)/E♭
Fma7
2.
A♭ma7(♭5)/E♭
D
Gmi7
fine
Solos
Ami7/D
Gma7
1.2.3.
A♭ma7(♭5)/E♭
Fma7
4.
A♭ma7(♭5)/E♭
Gmi7
Ami7
F/B♭
G/B
Cmi7
D7(♭13 ♯9)
Cue next
Interlude after solos
Ami7/D
Dma7/E♭
E♭ma7/F
Fma7/G
1. Gmi7
Fma7/A
Gma7/B
2. Gmi7
Fma7/A
Gma7/B
D.S. al fine

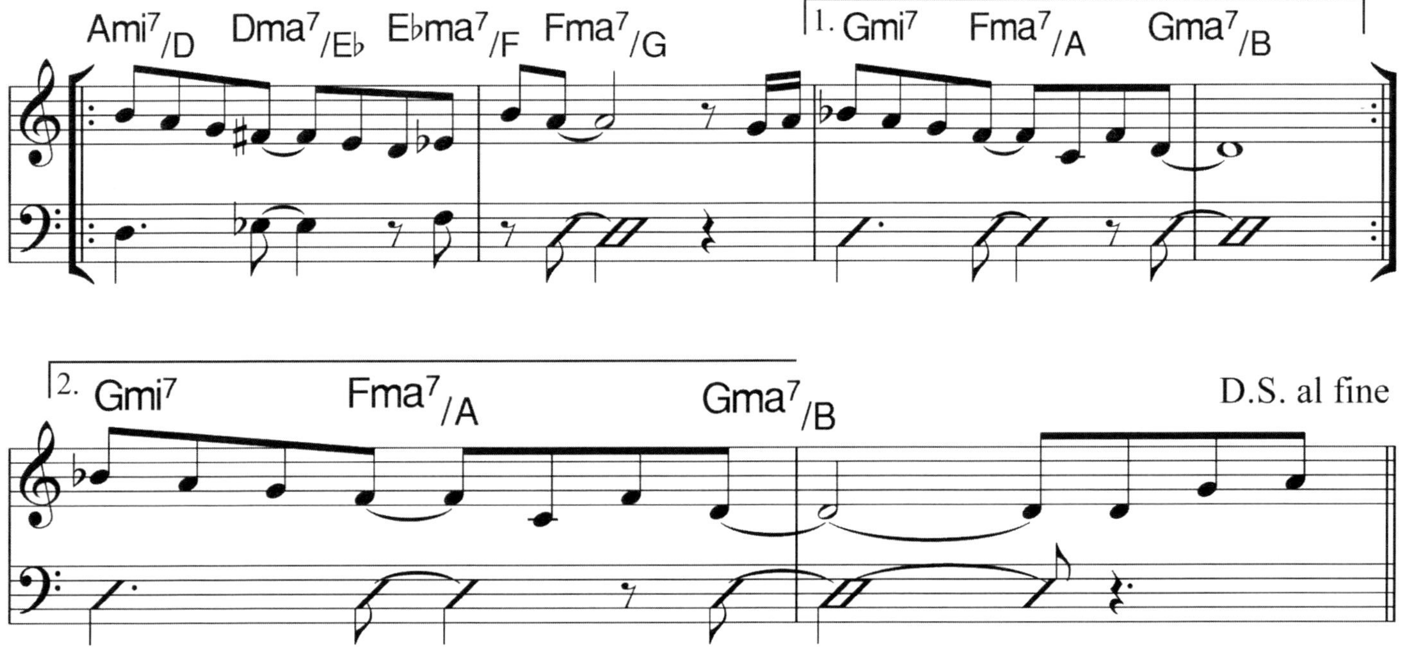

To Be

Ballad
Raimundo Santos
Intro
B♭ma13 E♭ma9 Dmi9 C9(sus)
If I could
A
B♭ma9 G♭+ B♭ma7 E♭ma9
see then I would know If I could breathe then I would live the way I
Instrumental solo . . .
Dmi7 C9(sus) B♭ma7
need the way I want my life to be
B
B♭ma9
If I could reach then I would
G♭+ B♭ma7 E♭ma9 Dmi7
grow If I could touch what seems so close for what I need for what I
C9(sus) B♭ma9
want my life to be
End solo
C
F13
Af - ter ma - ny bumps and brui - ses
E♭ma9 Dmi9 Cmi7
I'm still the one_ who los - es some - how I'm stand - ing so___ strong in___ the wrong_
E♭/F
D
B♭ma9 G♭+ B♭ma7
___ If I could walk then I would go or use my hands so they could
E♭ma7 Dmi7 C9(sus) B♭ma9
hold the things I need to live my life the way I want to be
1.
2.
E♭/G A♭ B♭ F/A Gmi B♭+/F B♭ma13(♯11)no3

To Lady

a tribute to Billie Holiday

Leon Mitchell

Recorded on: Max Roach Quintet "Quiet as It's Kept"/Mercury
www.leonmitchell.com

12
nev er sing songs that will bring us to tears once a- gain. Her-o-in be-came her shield from the world,
3
16
where she tried to lose the pain, but the pro-blems she found when ol' smack was a-round, just
20
made her life a liv-ing Hell. In her songs you can hear sad-ness, sel-dom much glad-ness 'cause her
24
songs told stor-ies of her own sad life. When she moan'd and she sigh'd all the feel-ings deep in-side came pour-ing

To Lady - 2

28
out and you knew just what La-dy was all a-bout. La-dy's stor-y had to come to an end.
32
Wish I could have been her friend, to sup-port and ad-vise, wipe the tears from her eyes, and

36
bring some com-fort TO LA-DY, to Bil-lie Hol-i-day, some

rit.
40
com-fort and peace to, some com-fort and peace to, some com-fort and peace TO LA-DY.
rit.

To the Roach

Up Tempo

Odean Pope

After Solos Repeat B to fine

Recorded on: Odean Pope, Saxophone Choir "To the Roach"/In and Out Records

www.odeanpope.com

Today

Aaron Graves

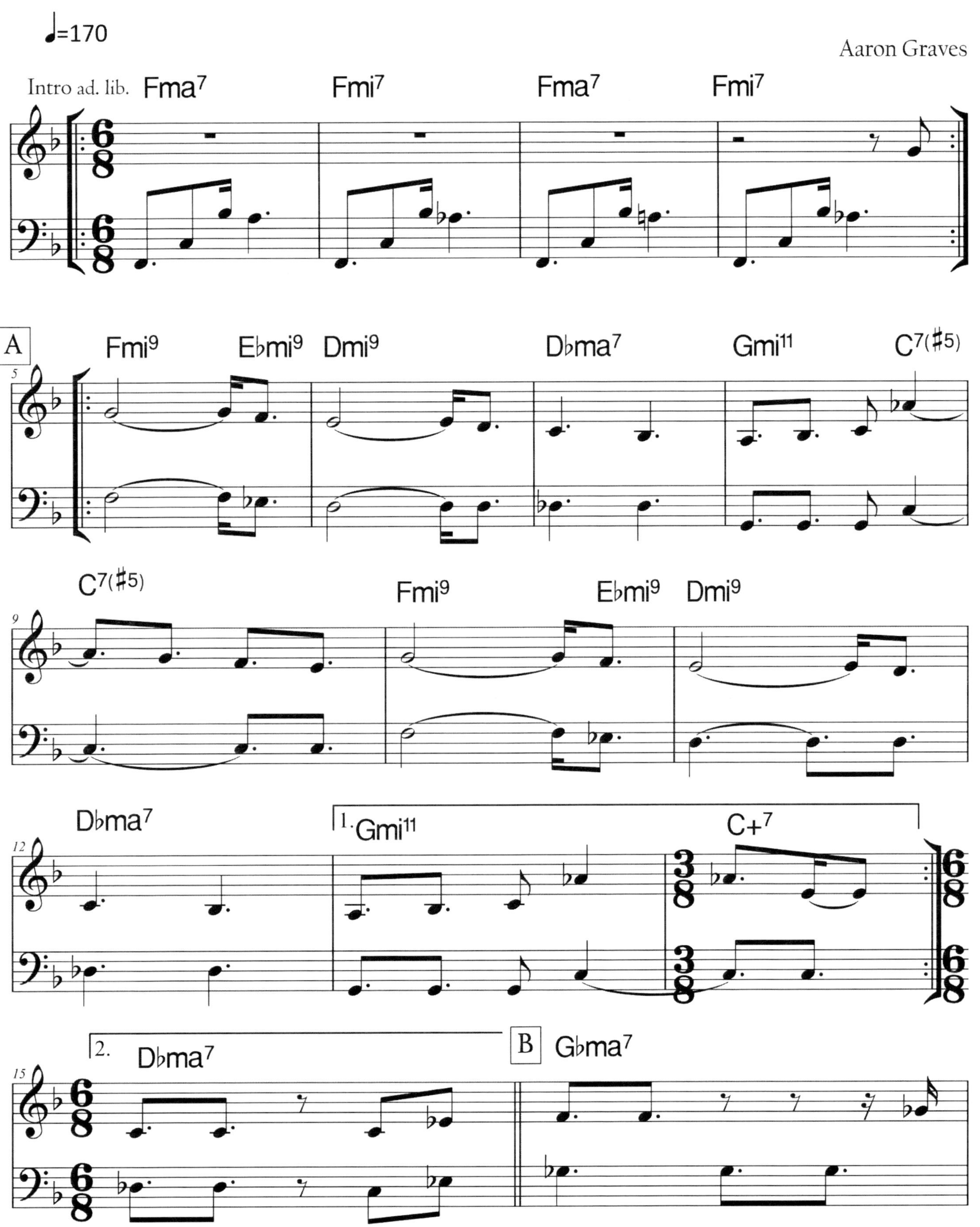

Play intro between Solos

Today - 2

Trane Ride

Eric Binder

Transcendence

from "City of Philadelphia, 2008"

Matt Davis

Recorded on: Matt Davis' Aerial Photograph "Ways and Means"/VanDolah Sounds

www.mattdavisguitar.com

© Two Beans Music/Published by Two Beans Music/Imani's Faith BMI
Recorded on: Barbara Montgomery "Trinity"/Two Beans Music BMI/Imani's Faith
www.bjazz.com www.aarongraves7.com

47
Cma7 Ami11 Gma7 Fma7(#11)
is your trin i ty
D
50
Bbma7 Bmi Ebma7(#11) Emi7 G#mi11 Ami
Past pre sent fu ture red white blue be ginn ing mid dle end
53
Bbma7(#9) Bmi Bbma7 Bmi Ebma7(#11) Emi9
Three wise men pat ience grace love win place show
56
G#mi11 Ami Bbma7 Dmi9
in ner out er oth er sis ter bro ther lov er
E
Solo
D(sus4)
59
D(sus4) F(sus4) D(sus4) D(sus4) Bbma7(#11)
66
Bmi11 Ebma7(#11) Emi11 Abmi(b13) Ami9
bo dy speech mind fa ther son ho ly ghost faith and hope de ceive
68
Bbma7 Bmi7 Bbma7 Bmi7 Ebma7 Emi9
what can you be lieve an ger de ludes de si re sun moon stars
71
Abma7 Ami9 D7(#9)
D.S. al Coda
pi an o bass drums three pass ions

F
D(sus4)
1.
Cma7 Ami11 Gma7 Fma7(♯11)
What
is your trin i ty
2.
Cma7 Ami11 Gma7 Fma7(♯11)
is your trin i ty
Samba
Solo Emi7
Emi7
G
Emi7
Mo ther fa ther child
I me mine
good bet ter best
Emi7
re nounce re pent re gret
Chris tian Mus lim Jew
a
Emi7
tone ac cept a noint
three bli nd mice
a to ss of the dice
and
Cma7
yet the quest ion waits with ser en i ty
and
Cma7
D(sus4)
still the quest ion lin gers in tran quil i ty
What
Cma7 Ami11 Gma7 Fma7(♯11)
is your trinity
D(sus4) Cma7 Gma7 Fma7(♯11)
What is your trin i ty

Troubled Times

Mark Kramer

Recorded on: Mark Kramer & Eddie Gomez "Troubled Times"/Eroica/Concord
www.mark-kramer.com

Tunnel

Terry Klinefelter

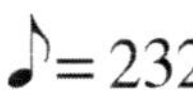

Vamp - (cont. thru A section) - straight 8ths

[cue next]

A

3

5

7

B Swing

C♯mi7 E♭mi7

11

1.

Emi7 C7(♯11)

15

2.

Emi7 F7

19

F7 F♯7 G7 A♭7 A7 (B♭)

21

D.C.

Recorded on: Terry Klinefelter "Zingaro"/Vectordisc
www.terryklinefelter.com

The Unifier

Recorded on: Joey DeFrancesco "Project Freedom"/Mack Avenue
www.joeydefrancesco.com

Up in Betty's Room

B
Dmi6
Emi7(♭5) A7
Dmi6
Emi7(♭5)
A7(♯9)
Dmi6
(Dmi6)
/D♭
Dmi7/C
B♭7
A7
Dmi6
D
E♭
C
Dmi6
solos:
(Emi7(5)
A7)
Dmi6
Emi7(♭5)
A7sus
Dmi6
/D♭
Dmi7/C
B♭7
A7
Dmi6
After Solos D.S. al Coda
walk
To Solos: 32 bar form from A.
Dmi6
B♭7
A7
Dmi6
B♭7
A7
G9(13)

Victory

Afro-Cuban

Robin Eubanks

Recorded on: Robin Eubanks & Steve Turre "Dedication"/JMT/Winter & Winter
www.robineubanks.com

perc. fill

perc. fill
Bbmi9
Emi9
A7/6
Abmaj9(#11)
Dmi9
Emi7
A9(b5)
Abmaj7/6
Eb/Db

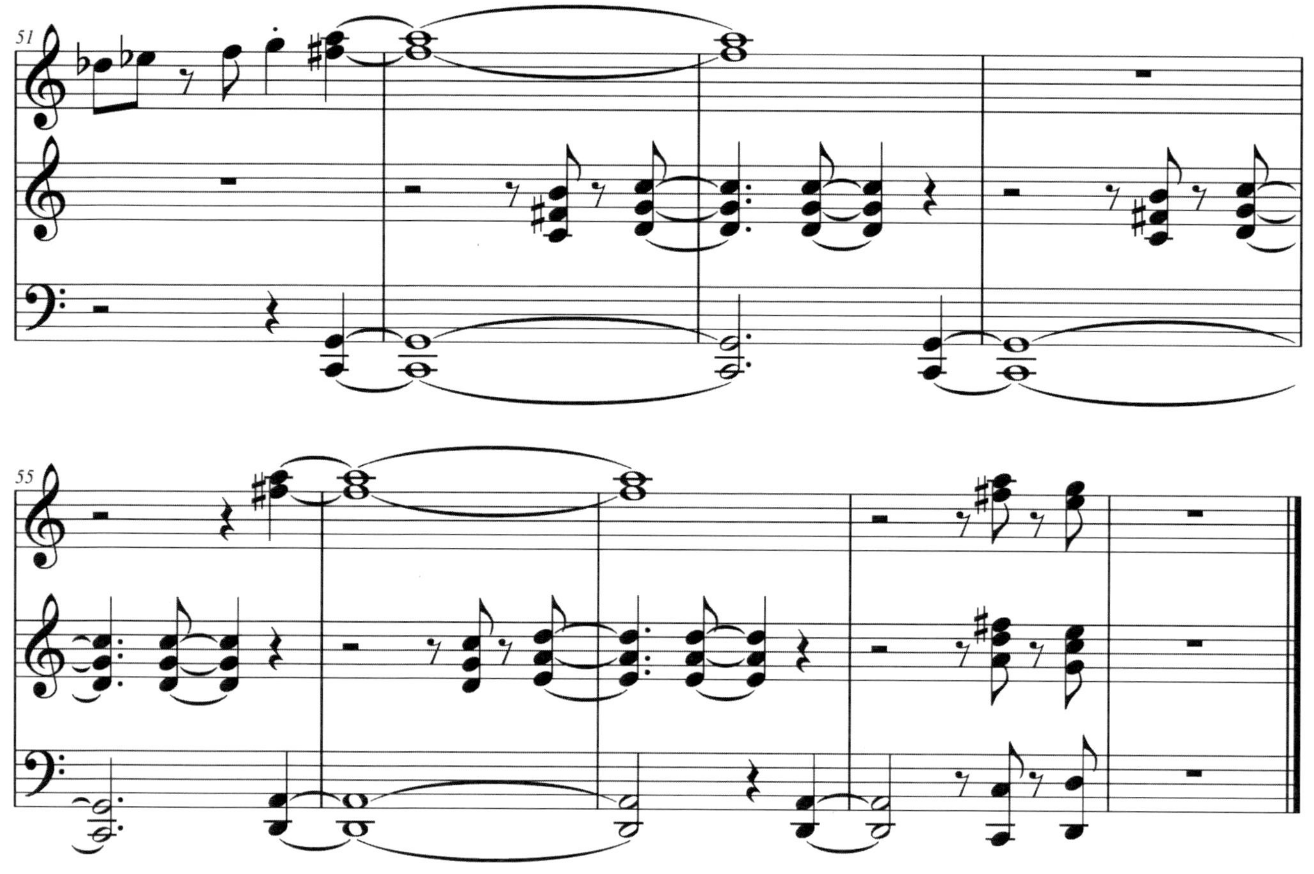

Solo changes

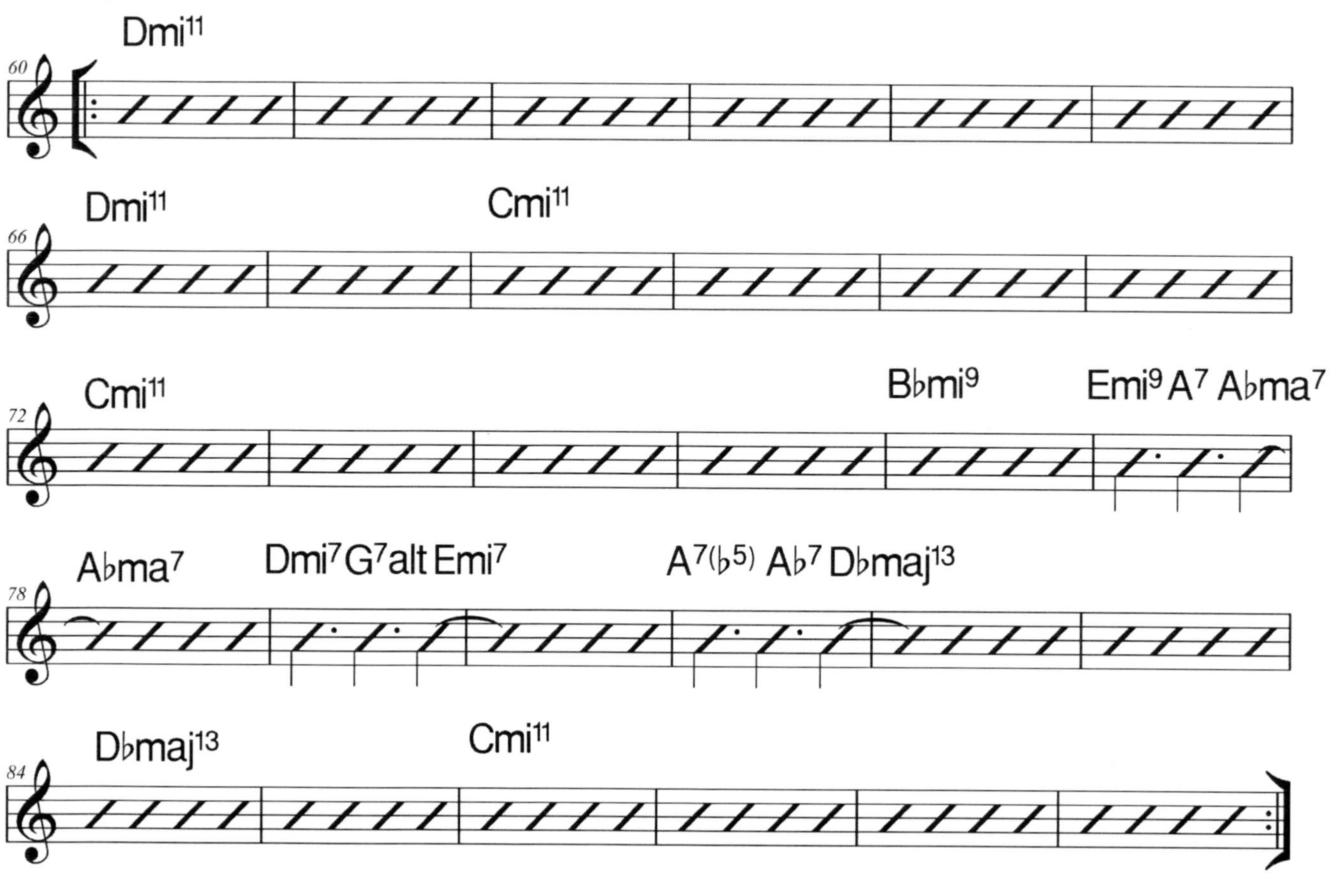

Vince Guaraldi

Tony Miceli

Recorded on: Diane Monroe Duo with Tony Miceli "Alone Together"/Dreambox Media
www.tonymiceli.com

35
Dmi7 A7 G7 E7 Ami7 E7
41
D7 G♭mi7(♭5) B7 Emi7 A7
47
Ami7 Gmi7 Fmi7 B♭9(sus4) B♭9 E♭ma7 E7
4
4
4
53
E♭ma7 A7(♯9 ♯5) A♭ma7 E♭/G F9
59
Fmi7 Dmi7(♭5) G7(♭9) Cmi7 F7(♭5) Fmi7 B♭9(sus4)
4
3
64
B♭7(♭9) Gmi7 C7(♯9 ♯5) C7(♭9) Fmi7 B♭9(sus4)
68
B♭9(sus4) B♭9 E♭ma7 Bma7 A♭7 Fmi7 B♭7

Warm Embraces

Denise Montana
& J. Siet

Recorded on: Denise Montana "In My Life"
www.denisemontana.com

We Miss You Sadly

Bobby Zankel

What's That?

Tony Miceli

Reocrded on: The Philly 5 "Looking East"/Miceli Music LLC, 2003
www.tonymiceli.com

Solos
Bmi7
Abmi7
Fmi7
Db9(#11)
Bb7(b9sus4)
Bb7(b9sus4)
Ebma7(#5)
Dmi7b5
G7(b9)
Cmi7
F9
G/A
Bma7/A#
B13
Bb13(b9)
1.
Ema7(b5)/D#
Ema7(b5)/D#
Gma7(b5)/F#
2.
Eb(sus4)
Eb
Abmi9
Bma7/A#
B°
F#mi7
G9(sus4)
F#(sus4)
F#
D/E
E/D
F/Db
G/C
Dbmi7
Ama7
Dbmi7
Ama7
Dbmi7
Ama7
F#mi7
F13
Bmi7
Abmi7
Fmi7
Db9(#11)
Bb7(b9sus4)
Bb7(b9)(sus4)
Ebma(#5)
Dmi7(b5)
G7(b9)
Cmi7
F9
G/A
Bma7/A#
B13
Bb13(b9)
Eb(sus4)
Eb
After solos D.C. al Coda

The Wicked Prosper

The Wizard of Montara

Recorded on: Christian McBride "Vertical Vision"/2003
www.christianmcbride.com

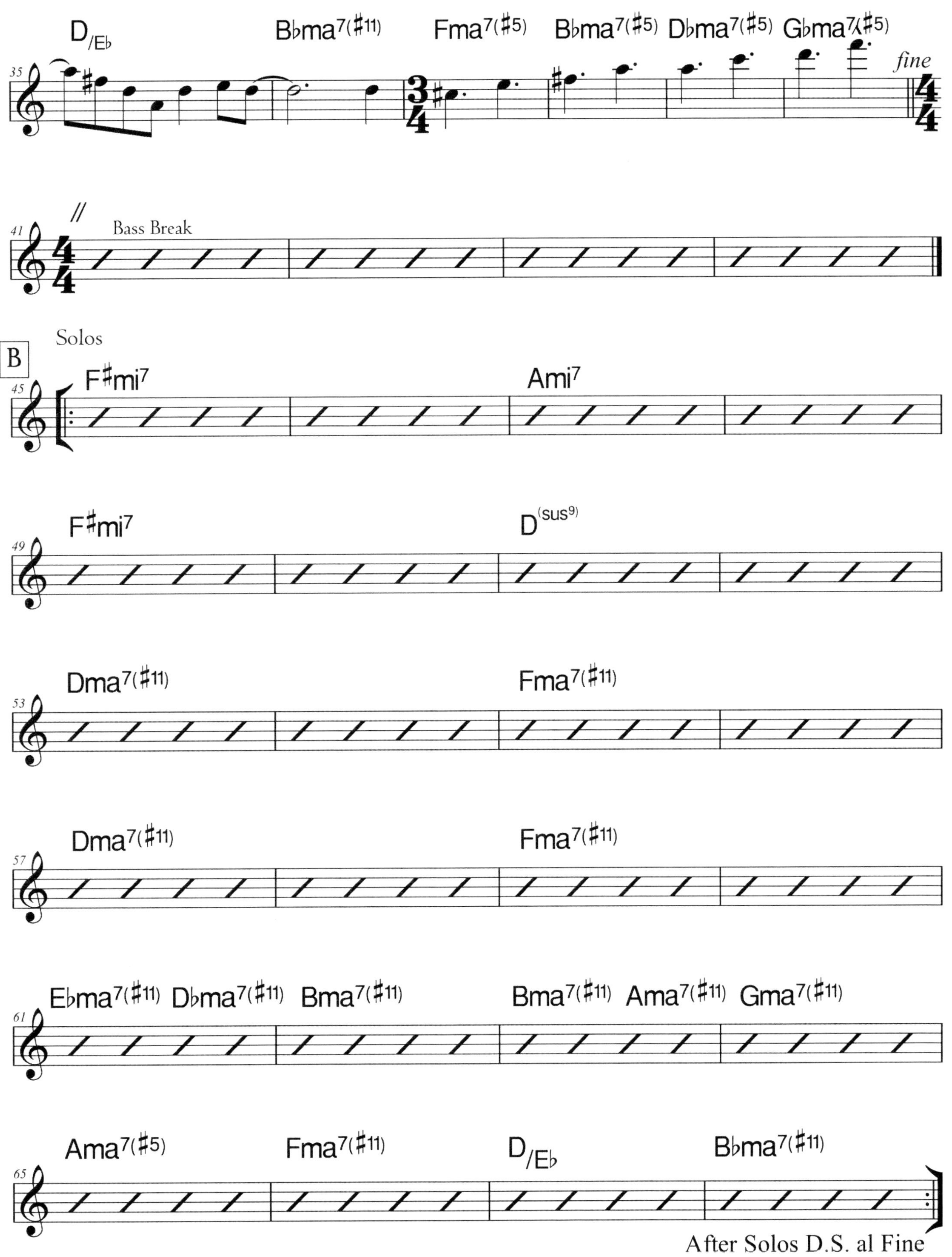
D/E♭
B♭ma7(♯11)
Fma7(♯5)
B♭ma7(♯5)
D♭ma7(♯5)
G♭ma7(♯5)
fine
Bass Break
B
Solos
F♯mi7
Ami7
F♯mi7
D(sus9)
Dma7(♯11)
Fma7(♯11)
Dma7(♯11)
Fma7(♯11)
E♭ma7(♯11)
D♭ma7(♯11)
Bma7(♯11)
Bma7(♯11)
Ama7(♯11)
Gma7(♯11)
Ama7(♯5)
Fma7(♯11)
D/E♭
B♭ma7(♯11)
After Solos D.S. al Fine

Woman Child

Recorded on: Chuck Anderson "The Vintage Tracks"/Anderson Music Productions Inc.
www.chuckandersonjazzguitar.com

Wonders Unfold

written for Nathan & Laura Distefano
for the occasion of their wedding, 2010

Contemp Jazz
Straight Eighths

David Dzubinski

www.brecherjazz.com/ddzubinski

The Words of Love

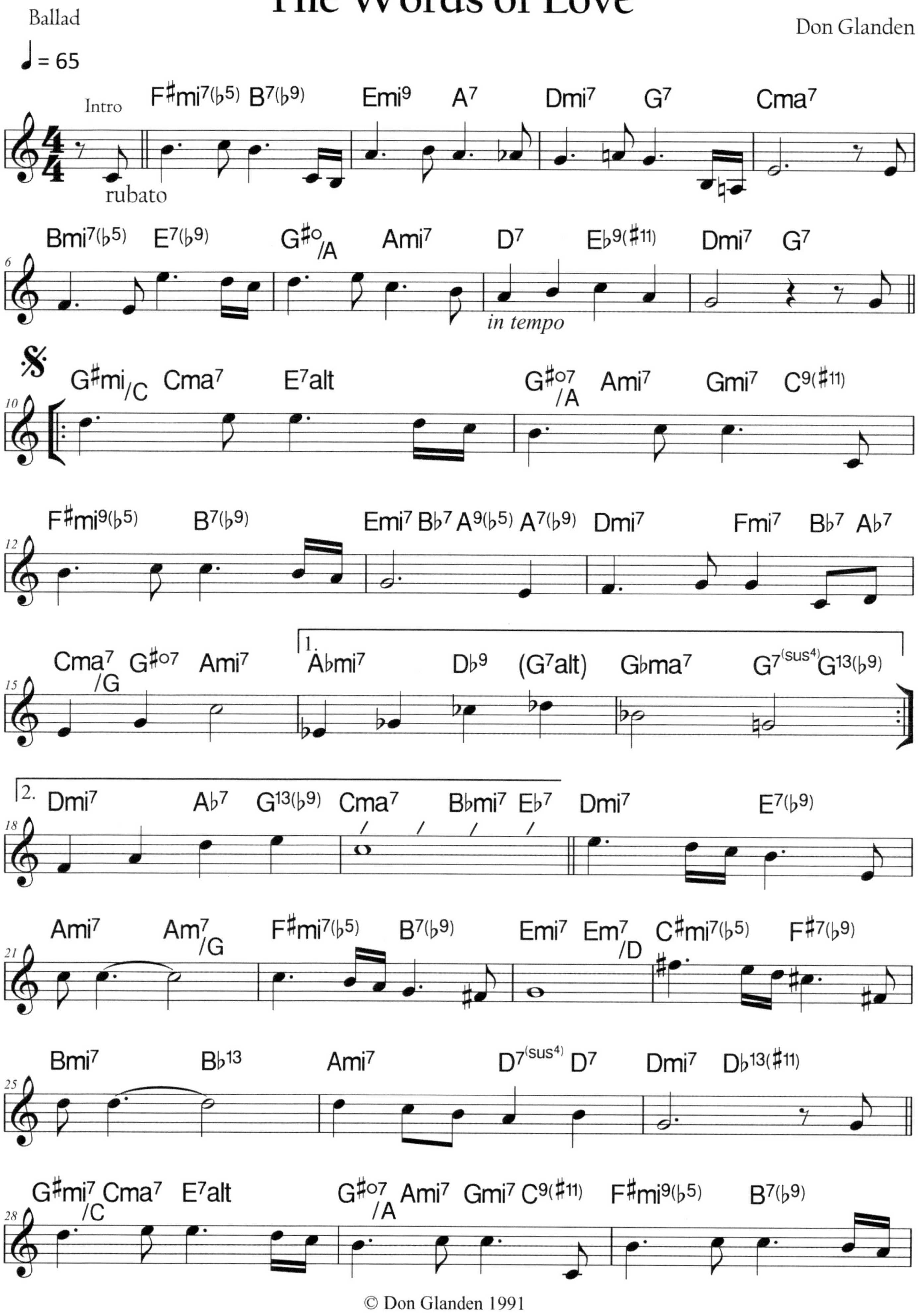

www.donglanden.com

After solos: D.S. al Fine

Zone 6
Medium
Straight Eighths
Marcell A. Bellinger
A
Cmi7
Cmi7/B♭
Ami7(♭5)
D7
Gmi Gmi/F♯ Gmi/F
C/E
F7
D/F♯
Gmi7
A♭ma7
Ami7
F♯mi7
Fmi7
E7(♯9)
E♭ma7
D♭ma7
break
Bma7
Play Time
B♭ma7
B
Bma7(♯11)
D♭ma7(♯11)
E♭ma7(♯11)
F13(sus4)
F13(♭9)
C
B♭mi7
B♭mi7/A♭
Gmi7(♭5)
C7
Fma7
B♭ma7
E♭ma7
A♭ma7
D♭ma7
F♯7(♯11)
Bma7
Ema7
G/A♭
Ama7(♯11)
Last time only

IN MEMORIAM

We honor those in *The Real Philadelphia Book* who shared their compositions but who are no longer with us.

Morris "Mo" Bailey
Robert "Bootsie" Barnes
John Blake, Jr.
Ray Bryant
William "Mr. C." Carney
Father John D'Amico
Charles Fambrough
Paul Gehman
Eddie Green
Jimmy Heath
Billy James
Jef Lee Johnson
Philly Joe Jones
Byard Lancaster
Jymie Merritt
George Mesterhazy
Jim Miller
Hank Mobley
Lee Morgan
Don Patterson
Trudy Pitts
Shirley Scott
James "Sid" Simmons
Keno Speller
Bob Timmons
Grover Washington, Jr.

JAZZ BRIDGE
THE REAL PHILADELPHIA BOOK
2nd Edition

jazz bridge

JAZZ BRIDGE PROJECT gratefully acknowledges that partial funding for ***The Real Philadelphia Book*** project was provided by generous contributions from the following:

Keswick Theatre

Rhenda Fearrington

Rob Frederick

Bassist Bert Harris

Alfred Harrison

Carol Rogers

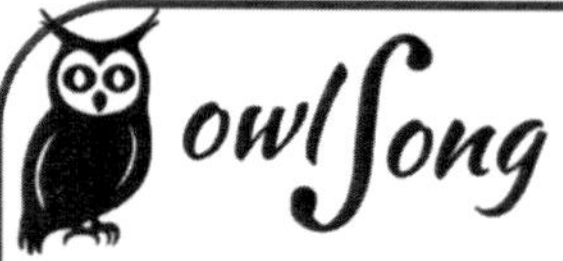

A unique blend of jazz, Latin, classical, medieval, flamenco, mideastern ...

Alan Lewine
&
Ana María
Ruimonte

You've never heard anything like this before!

Soprano Meets Bass
Sephardic Treasures

Latest release on Ansonica Records

More info on this and other releases at **www.owlsong.com**

Owlsong Productions • email: info@owlsong.com

"Congrats Jazz Bridge on this great collection of Philly Jazz!"

Design by Kathy Ridl